2250

The Dow Jones-Irwin Guide
to Investing with Investment Software

The Dow Jones-Irwin Guide to Investing with Investment Software

Thomas A. Meyers

DOW JONES-IRWIN
Homewood, Illinois 60430

© DOW JONES-IRWIN, 1987

ISBN 0-87094-938-1
Library of Congress Catalog Card No. 86–71442

Printed in the United States of America

1 2 3 4 5 6 7 8 9 0 K 4 3 2 1 0 9 8 7

For Marianne

Preface

The widespread use of personal computers is leading to fundamental changes in the way investors obtain and use information. With investment software, you can easily monitor your portfolio, screen databases containing thousands of stocks to find those that meet predefined investment criteria, generate scores of technical market indicators, and perform complex technical analysis on individual securities.

This book shows you how to take advantage of computerized investing capabilities. You will learn how to use the three major types of investment software—portfolio management, fundamental analysis, and technical analysis software. In addition, software that can be used for options analysis is discussed.

This book is not a directory of investment software, nor is it a collection of software reviews. Rather it illustrates in detail the best ways to utilize the various types of investment software and provides specific guidance on how to select an investment software package that will meet your needs.

The software packages used for illustration represent, in my opinion, the best investment software packages available at the time this book was written. For consistency, the IBM® PC version of each software package was used.

For those interested in further information on one of the software packages referred to in this book, Appendix B contains the vendor's address and telephone number. The price of each software package is also noted. However, prices may be lower by the time you read this book.

If you are a serious investor, using investment software can improve your chances of making profitable investment decisions. With personal computers and investment software at their lowest prices ever, there is no better time to take advantage of computerized investing capabilities. This book provides a starting point.

Tom Meyers

Contents

Analysis Software: *The Technician. MetaStock. CompuTrac/PC. Telescan—An On-Line Alternative. A Warning.* Conclusion.

Do Investors Really Need Personal Computers?

A couple of years ago, computer mania was in full swing. News stories told us that soon there would be a personal computer in every home. We were promised that these magnificent machines would do everything from balancing our checkbooks to making our morning coffee.

Well, the rosy computer sales projections of a couple of years ago have fallen prey to reality. Skeptics are even telling us that computer sales are on the decline and that maybe, just maybe, not everyone needs a personal computer.

As usual, reality exists somewhere between the two extremes. Has the growth in computer sales met the expectations of a couple of years ago? Clearly, it has not. Has the growth been substantial and will it continue to be so? Absolutely.

According to one major market research firm, the number of personal computers in the home grew from 6.3 million to 10 million from year-ends 1983 to 1984, and to 13.7 million at the end of 1985. More than a 100 percent increase in personal computer sales in two years is no small achievement.

Furthermore, and probably more important, a greater percentage of home personal computers are higher priced units, such as the Apple® II series and IBM® PC, as opposed to the lower priced Commodore 64. Thus, the capabilities of the average home computer have increased.

What does all of this mean to investors? How many of them are using personal computers? Surveys estimate that 10 percent of personal computers in the home are currently being used for investment analysis.

Given the likelihood that more and more individuals will be using personal computers for investment purposes as time goes on, should you rush out and buy one if you haven't already? It depends on your style of investing.

If you blindly follow your broker's advice regarding what to buy and sell and when to do so, you probably do not need a personal computer, at least not for investment purposes. On the other hand, if you are more independent and prefer to perform your own investment research and analysis, a personal computer will be tremendously valuable throughout the investment process—from identifying securities to buy and sell, to placing orders on-line, to monitoring securities after purchase.

Before considering which personal computer model to buy, first identify the specific software you plan to use with it. A personal computer can be an expensive paper weight if it won't run the type of software you want to use.

In general, if you plan to use a personal computer for investment purposes and insist on buying it before you identify specific software packages, an Apple II series computer or an IBM PC is your best bet. A substantial amount of investment software exists for both models as well as for the true IBM PC compatibles.

As an investor, what type of software will you be able to find? There are three primary types of investment software—portfolio management, fundamental analysis, and technical analysis software.

PORTFOLIO MANAGEMENT SOFTWARE

Portfolio management software packages are the simplest to use and easiest to understand of the investment software packages. They do not encompass all of the tasks normally associated with managing a portfolio of securities, but they organize key portfolio information and generate a variety of portfolio status reports. In other words, they are basically accounting packages.

Using one of these packages involves entering information on the securities you own or want to follow into one or more portfolios, pricing out your holdings by manual input of current security prices or automatic update from an on-line service, and generating various reports on your holdings. Typically, these packages enable you to generate current portfolio status, profit and loss statements, individual security status, dividend income, and interest income reports. In addition, reports often provide advance notice of stocks going long-term, dividends coming due, and options expiring.

Part 2 of this book is devoted to portfolio management software. There you will find guidance on selecting and using portfolio management software, using spreadsheet programs to monitor your investments, and managing your portfolio on-line.

FUNDAMENTAL ANALYSIS SOFTWARE

On to the fundamentalists. Do they have anything to cheer about when it comes to using personal computers. They certainly do.

Fundamentalists typically identify buy and sell opportunities by looking at the underlying value of securities. One way to do so is to evaluate a group of securities and identify those meeting a predefined set of criteria.

For example, a fundamentalist might look for stocks listed on the New York Stock Exchange with a market price less than book value per share. Alternatively, he may want to locate stocks with a price/earnings ratio less than 10, a yield greater than 10 percent, and an increase in sales from the prior year of greater than 10 percent. It will take hours to identify such stocks manually.

However, in a matter of seconds, a stock screening software package can accomplish the same task and extract a short, specific list of the stocks meeting the predefined investment criteria. That's right—seconds!

Using a stock screening software package, you can request a list of stocks meeting multiple criteria. The software will search through a database containing information on thousands of stocks and provide a list of those meeting your criteria. Obviously, manipulating large amounts of data is one of the things personal computers do best.

Part 3 of this book describes how to select and use fundamental analysis software to screen for stocks meeting a predefined set of investment criteria and how to analyze individual companies. A chapter is also devoted to obtaining important company information from on-line services.

TECHNICAL ANALYSIS SOFTWARE

What about the technicians, otherwise known as elves? Are personal computers valuable to them? They certainly are. In fact, technical analysis software packages are the most popular of the investment software packages—and with good reason.

Imagine that you want to graph a stock's price for the last year—not just the closing price, but also the high and low. On top of that, imagine that you want to calculate and plot a 50-day moving average of the closing price on the same chart. How much time will it take you? Certainly hours, if not days, depending on whether you have all of the stock prices at hand. Now imagine that you can do the same thing in less than five minutes using technical analysis software.

Virtually all of the time-consuming task of preparing charts can be eliminated by using technical analysis software. In a matter of a few minutes and with relative ease, you can automatically retrieve the current and historical price and volume data from an on-line database and create a chart that includes a security's high-low price range, closing price, time frame (hours, days, weeks), volume, various moving averages, momentum indices, oscillators, and more. And, as opposed to subscribing to expensive publications containing stock and commodity charts that never seem to arrive on time, your charts will always reflect current market conditions.

Part 4 of this book provides guidance on selecting and using technical analysis software. Generating technical market indicators, charting individual securities, and testing trading strategies are covered in depth.

OPTIONS SOFTWARE

Options traders will be happy to know that they haven't been left out. There are numerous options software packages available to help analyze both simple and complex option positions. However, when looking at these packages, make sure you know which option valuation model (e.g., Black-Scholes) is being used. Otherwise, you could end up with software that evaluates options using a method you don't agree with.

Part 5 of this book describes how to select and use options software.

ON-LINE SERVICES

In addition to using investment software, investors can hook up to on-line databases via telephone lines to instantly access current and historical quotes, up-to-the-minute news, consensus earnings forecasts, insider trading information, company financial statements, and a wealth of other financial information. Electronic advisory services allow you to query investment experts on-line, and a growing number of brokerage firms now allow you to enter stock orders directly through your computer.

On-line services are an integral part of using any type of investment software. They are discussed throughout the book.

With all these fantastic capabilities available, why aren't more investors taking advantage of them? There are several reasons.

OVERCOMING DETERRENTS TO USING INVESTMENT SOFTWARE

First and foremost, some people are intimidated by computers. Fortunately, with a few hours at the keyboard of a personal computer, this fear can quickly be overcome. Personal computers and software have evolved to the point where they are truly easy to use. Many software packages require only a few keystrokes to perform the tasks you require.

A second deterrent is the entry cost. A typical personal computer system costs between $1,500 and $3,000. Add to that the cost of software packages averaging from $300 to $500 each, and many individuals simply cannot justify the cost given the size of their portfolios. The good news is that the price of personal computer systems and software continues to decrease and will be much more affordable in the near future.

A final road block is the scarcity of information on investment software. Although there are hundreds of investment software packages to choose from, locating software that meets your personal investment needs can be like going through a maze. Virtually all investment software packages are sold only through the mail. Thus, you cannot go to your local computer store for a demonstration or even for more information.

The only way to locate many software packages is to flip through various computer and financial publications and hope that you stumble across an advertisement for software meeting your needs. This, of course, can be time-consuming and frustrating. And, when you do find a software package, you have to think twice before paying several hundred dollars in advance for something that you have not seen demonstrated and cannot return for a refund if it is not what you want.

This book solves that problem by providing the key information you need to know when selecting investment software. It also directs you to sources that publish comprehensive and ongoing reviews of investment software packages and regularly updated directories of investment software.

Are personal computers worth the cost to investors? Many successful investors feel they are. After reading this book, you will be able to decide for yourself.

PART 1

Getting Started

CHAPTER 1

Hardware: What You Need to Know

If you are like most investors, you want to take advantage of the capabilities that investment software packages offer, but you are not particularly interested in the mechanics of how a personal computer allows you to do so. Fortunately, there are only a few things you need to know to get started.

COMPONENTS OF A PERSONAL COMPUTER SYSTEM

A personal computer system useful for investment purposes typically consists of six components: the system unit, disk drives, keyboard, monitor, printer, and modem.

The system unit is the core of the personal computer system. It includes the electronic circuits and microchips that make the computer work and the memory used to process the programmed instructions provided by the software. All other components of the system are attached to the system unit.

The disk drives are used to input information into the system unit. Programmed instructions and data to be processed are transferred from a magnetic floppy disk to the computer's memory. Then, after the data is processed by the computer, it is transferred back to a floppy disk, saving the processed results for later use. Disk drives operate very much like a cassette tape recorder.

The computer's keyboard is also used for input. It looks like the keypad on a typewriter but includes additional special-purpose keys known as function keys.

Using the keyboard, you enter the instructions required to start and run a specific program. You can also enter data to be used by the program.

The monitor, similar to a television screen, is used to see text and graphics. Two types of monitors, monochrome and color, are available. For investment purposes monochrome monitors are usually sufficient. However, you may find a color monitor beneficial when using certain technical analysis software packages.

The printer is used to retain text and graphics as a permanent record. There are several different types of printers available, but for investment purposes the choice is clearly a dot matrix printer. Dot matrix printers connect a series of small dots together to form characters and print graphs.

The final component, the modem, is a device that allows you to send and receive information over telephone lines. The modem is used when you want to retrieve information, such as current stock quotes and company news, from an on-line service like Dow Jones News/Retrieval.®

SOME SPECIFIC ADVICE

Now that you know the basic components of a personal computer system, how do you choose one to buy?

First of all, you need a personal computer that will run the type of software you want to use, in this case, investment software. The vast majority of investment software will run only on Apple II series and the IBM PC, XT, or AT (or true IBM PC compatibles). There are only a few investment software packages available for other personal computers, such as the Commodore 64, and the capabilities of the best of such software are limited. Therefore, for practical purposes you have only two choices.

Many investment software packages require a minimum of 128K memory to operate on an Apple II series computer or 256K memory to operate on an IBM PC, XT, or AT (or true compatibles). The standard systems you are likely to buy already contain the minimum memory requirements.

If you are using anything other than portfolio management software, you will likely need two floppy disk drives or one floppy disk drive along with a hard disk drive. Like the floppy disk drive, the hard disk drive is an input/output device. But it is much faster and can store many times as much information as can be stored on a floppy disk. I recommend that you start off with two floppy disk drives. You can always add a hard disk drive to the system at a later time when your needs are better known.

Monitors can be monochrome or color. Color may be aesthetically pleasing, but it adds little to the functionality of the system. If you are using portfolio management or fundamental analysis software, you definitely do not need a color monitor— the less costly monochrome monitor is sufficient.

If you plan to use technical analysis software, you may find a color monitor helpful in distinguishing the various elements of a graph. For example, if you plot two moving averages on a chart of a stock's price over a given period of time, having each plotted in a different color may make interpretation easier. However, most technicians find a monochrome monitor adequate.

Investment software sends programmed instructions to the printer, and each printer requires a predefined set of instructions to operate properly. Software vendors normally include operating instructions for only the best selling printers. I recommend the Epson® dot matrix printer (or one that is compatible). Epson is the standard of dot matrix printers and will operate with the vast majority of investment software.

A final consideration is the modem. Speed of transmission and reliability are concerns here. Transmission speeds are quoted in terms of baud rates. For example, a 1200-baud modem can send and receive data four times as fast as a 300-baud modem.

Transmission speeds keep increasing and are expected to reach 9600-baud during the next few years. For now, buy a modem that has a minimum transmission speed of 1200-baud. Hayes® modems are industry standards and should be seriously considered.

Where should you buy your hardware? Shop around just like you would for a television set. I saved as much as 40 percent on a modem and 30 percent on a printer by making a few telephone calls. In most cases, the hardware needs little servicing and the same warranties apply regardless of where you purchase it.

A FINAL NOTE

The costs of personal computer systems have and will continue to decrease dramatically as time goes on. Select your hardware carefully, based on what you want it to do using investment and other types of software, and it will serve you well.

CHAPTER 2

Evaluating Investment Software

With over 500 investment software packages to choose from, locating software that meets your investment needs can be difficult. But, in the long run, it is worthwhile to locate a package that allows your personal computer to perform repetitive and time-consuming tasks such as chart preparation and stock screening because that leaves you more time to concentrate on interpreting the results.

Due to the specialized nature of investment software, a local computer store probably won't be able to provide any assistance in the selection process. The majority of investment software is available only through the mail, and the buyer must beware. In many cases, you must pay several hundred dollars in advance for software that you have not even seen demonstrated, and once you open the package, it cannot be returned for a refund. For this reason alone, it is important to research and investigate each package as thoroughly as possible before buying.

Another factor to remember in your search for investment software is that everyone invests differently. We all have different levels of stress, different temperaments, and different amounts of capital. Some of us can afford to lose money, while others are on a tight budget. It is important to locate a package that complements your personality and individual investment philosophy. Otherwise, you will not receive the benefits you are looking for from one of these packages.

DEVELOPING A CHECKLIST OF KEY FEATURES

Before choosing an investment software package, make a list of criteria that you feel are absolutely necessary. Be specific. For example, if you are accustomed to using point and figure charts with $1 per unit and three units per reversal, write it down. If you use specific indicators or oscillators, write down what they are and how you calculate them. This process takes some time, but the finished list can be used to help evaluate alternatives. The checklist can reflect what you currently do without the aid of investment software, as well as whatever you want to do.

You could also use the extensive questionnaires provided in Chapter 3 (for portfolio management software), Chapter 6 (for fundamental analysis software), Chapter 9 (for technical analysis software), and Chapter 12 (for options software). These questionnaires help you focus on the important elements of each type of software and provide an easy way to compare one software package with another.

BEGINNING YOUR SEARCH FOR INVESTMENT SOFTWARE

With your personalized checklist or one of the questionnaires in hand, you can begin your search. First, identify vendors who have a product that might meet your needs. A good start is to review an up-to-date directory of investment software, such as the one in Appendix A. In addition, look through various computer and financial publications for advertisements that provide the names and addresses of vendors.

The next step is to contact each vendor and request general information on its products. With this information, you will eliminate many packages that do not meet your criteria.

There are several ways to screen the remaining packages to eliminate those that do not meet your needs. You can talk to other users of the package and inquire how long they have used it, what problems, if any, they have experienced in using it, and how they like it. You can also look for an independent review of the package. Reviews in computer and financial publications provide valuable information regarding how well various software packages function.

In many cases, you can also purchase a demonstration package for a nominal amount, usually $10 or less. If you subsequently purchase the software package, this amount will often be deducted from the cost of the package. The demonstration package normally contains a disk and written material that illustrates in detail the various features of the software package.

After this process, you will have narrowed down your choices significantly. One last thing to do before making a final decision is to call the vendor and review your checklist or questionnaire in detail to ensure that the package does everything you want it to do.

Many investors use more than one software package to meet all of their investment needs, and you probably will too. For example, you may require a portfolio management software package and a stock screening package. In addition, you may use a spreadsheet program, such as Lotus 1-2-3®.

CONCLUSION

Locating investment software that complements your style of investing can be difficult but, in the long run, is worth the effort. Throughout this book, you will find examples of some of the best software packages available. These and others will perform the repetitive and time-consuming tasks of investing, leaving you more time to concentrate on making the best possible investment decisions.

PART 2

Portfolio Management

CHAPTER 3

Portfolio Management Software

One of the keys to successful investing is keeping a close eye on your investments. Are they going up or down in value? How does their performance compare to other types of investments?

Monitoring your portfolio is not a difficult task in itself. It involves pricing out your holdings at their current value and evaluating each individual investment and the portfolio as a whole using different performance measures. How often you review your portfolio depends on the types of investments you own and whether you take a short- or long-term approach to investing.

Monitoring your portfolio does involve time-consuming mathematical calculations and manipulation of key portfolio information. Fortunately, personal computers are well suited for this type of activity. Using a personal computer with portfolio management software, calculations can be performed quickly and accurately, and key information can be manipulated into a variety of reports to give you the information you need to properly review your holdings.

There are two major types of portfolio management software packages. One type is geared to the individual investor, while the other focuses on the needs of the professional, such as a stockbroker or money manager. In addition, some software packages can be used by both individual and professional investors.

SELECTING PORTFOLIO MANAGEMENT SOFTWARE

A number of considerations should be made in selecting a portfolio management software package to meet your needs. A good way to compare alternative packages is to complete a questionnaire like the one in Exhibit 3–1 for each package. By doing so, you ensure that you have considered all of the important factors in evaluating portfolio management software packages.

Remember, to make sure you purchase software that meets your individual needs, you must take time to evaluate a number of packages before making your final decision. In the long run, the benefit you receive from using the right package will make this process worth the effort.

EXHIBIT 3–1   Portfolio Management Software Questionnaire—IBM PC Systems

---

GENERAL INFORMATION

Product name: _____   Version #: _____
Vendor name: _____
Address: _____
               _____
               _____
Telephone: _____
List price: _____
Demonstration diskette available?   _____ Yes   _____ No
    If yes, what is the price of the demonstration diskette? _____
Money-back guarantee available?   _____ Yes   _____ No
    If yes, how many days? _____

HARDWARE REQUIREMENTS

Operating system: _____ DOS 1.1 or later   _____Other (Specify) _____
                 _____ DOS 2.0 or later
Minimum memory required: _____ 64K   _____ 128K   _____ 192K   _____ 256K
Number of disk drives required: _____ 1 single-sided
                                  _____ 2 single-sided
                                  _____ 1 double-sided
                                  _____ 2 double-sided
                            Other _____
Color graphics required?   _____ Yes   _____ No
Modem required?   _____ Yes   _____ No
Modem recommended?   _____ Yes   _____ No
Printer required?   _____ Yes   _____ No
Printer recommended?   _____ Yes   _____ No
Other hardware requirements (specify): _____
_____
_____
_____

PRODUCT SUPPORT

Who provides support for the product? _____
Is there a telephone number available for support?   _____ Yes   _____ No
    If yes, is it toll-free?   _____ Yes   _____ No
    Days of the week support is available: _____
    Hours of the day support is available: _____

EXHIBIT 3–1 (*continued*)

Is the software copy protected? _____ Yes _____ No
If yes, can you copy program to a hard disk? _____ Yes _____ No
Cost of backup copy? _____
Defective disk replacement policy: _____
_____
_____
_____

Update policy: _____
_____
_____

DOCUMENTATION

Number of pages in user's manual? _____
User's manual includes: Yes No
  Tutorial _____ _____
  Index _____ _____
  Glossary _____ _____
  Explanation of error messages _____ _____
  Sample applications _____ _____
  Samples of screen displays _____ _____
  Samples of printed output _____ _____
Does the package include a tutorial on disk? _____ Yes _____ No
Does the package include a reference card? _____ Yes _____ No
Does the disk contain sample applications? _____ Yes _____ No
  If yes, how many and what type? _____
Does the package include a demonstration disk? _____ Yes _____ No

EASE OF USE

Estimated time to learn basic functions:
  _____ Less than 1 day _____ 1 to 6 days _____ 1 to 2 weeks
  _____ Over 2 weeks
Commands are abbreviated for quick entry? _____ Yes _____ No
Error messages are provided on screen? _____ Yes _____ No
Programs are menu driven? _____ Yes _____ No
Help screens are available? _____ At all times
                             _____ At various points in the program
                             _____ Nonexistent
How experienced with the IBM PC should a person be to use this package?
  _____ Very _____ Somewhat _____ Little _____ No experience

SECURITY TYPES

Which of the following types of securities can be maintained in a portfolio?
  (Check all that apply)
  _____ Common stocks   _____ Options
  _____ Preferred stocks   _____ Warrants
  _____ Corporate bonds   _____ Commodities
  _____ Municipal bonds   _____ Futures
  _____ U.S. Treasury bonds   _____ Other (Specify) _____
        and notes
  _____ Convertible bonds   _____ Other (Specify) _____
  _____ Mutual funds

EXHIBIT 3–1   (*continued*)

DATA ENTRY

Is the user prompted for data to be entered?   _____ Yes   _____ No
Which of the following items are entered? (Check all that apply)
_____ Security symbol   _____ Purchase price or sell value
                                                    (per share or total)
_____ Security description   _____ Ex-dividend date
_____ Security classification   _____ Dividend rate
_____ Transaction date   _____ Yield
_____ Quantity bought   _____ Margined positions
_____ Quantity sold   _____ Margin interest rate
_____ Commission   _____ Current market price per unit
_____ Other (Specify) _____
_____ Other (Specify) _____
Can the user access an on-line database for current price updates?
_____ Yes   _____ No
If yes, which on-line database is accessed? (Check all that apply)
_____ Dow Jones News/Retrieval
_____ Warner Computer Systems
_____ Other (Specify) _____
_____ Other (Specify) _____
Does the software allow for entry of fractional prices?   _____ Yes   _____ No
Does the software allow for entry of the maturity date of bonds?
_____ Yes   _____ No
Does the software allow for the entry of option expiration dates?
_____ Yes   _____ No
Can the user record short sales?   _____ Yes   _____ No
Can the user record the writing of covered calls and puts?
_____ Yes   _____ No
Can the user record margined positions?   _____ Yes   _____ No
After data is entered, can it be easily checked and changed?
_____ Yes   _____ No

FEATURES

What is the maximum number of portfolios per disk? _____
What is the maximum number of securities per portfolio? _____
What is the maximum number of transactions per security? _____
Can the user classify securities into fixed categories?
_____ Yes   _____ No
Can the user classify securities into user-definable categories?
_____ Yes   _____ No
Can items be cross-referenced between portfolios?   _____ Yes   _____ No
If yes, which of the following items can be cross-referenced? (Check all
that apply)
_____ Security symbol
_____ Number of shares
_____ Purchase price
_____ Percentage gain or loss
_____ Other (Specify) _____
_____ Other (Specify) _____

EXHIBIT 3–1 *(continued)*

Can securities be sorted by type? _____ Yes _____ No
Can securities be sorted alphabetically? _____ Yes _____ No
Can securities be sorted by date of purchase? _____ Yes _____ No
Are sells matched with previous buys? _____ Yes _____ No
Is the update of one security in one portfolio transferred to all
    portfolios? _____ Yes _____ No

REPORTS

Can reports be generated on the screen? _____ Yes _____ No
Can reports be printed? _____ Yes _____ No
Which of the following types of reports can be generated? (Check all that apply)
    _____ Current portfolio status report
    _____ Cash portfolio status report
    _____ Dividend/bond interest due report
    _____ Dividend income report
    _____ Individual security status report
    _____ Long-term status report
    _____ Interest income report
    _____ Tax year profit/loss report
    _____ Other (Specify) _____
Which of the following items do reports display? (Check all that apply)
    _____ Security description
    _____ Purchase date
    _____ Quantity purchased
    _____ Latest market price per unit
    _____ Current value of each security
    _____ Total current value of portfolio
    _____ Unrealized gains and losses
    _____ Stock position—long or short
    _____ Holdings about to go long-term
    _____ Holdings nearing user-defined high-price limits
    _____ Holdings nearing user-defined low-price limits
    _____ Commissions and fees paid when security purchased
    _____ Calculated commissions to be paid when position is closed
    _____ Dividends received per security
    _____ Percentage yield on purchase cost
    _____ Percentage yield on current value
    _____ Percentage of each security to the total portfolio
    _____ Short-term gain or loss per transaction
    _____ Long-term gain or loss per transaction
    _____ Other (Specify) _____
    _____ Other (Specify) _____

CLIENT INFORMATION (Complete this section only if software is intended to
    be used by professionals to manage client portfolios.)
Which of the following items are maintained for each client? (Check all that
    apply)
    _____ Name
    _____ Address
    _____ Telephone number

EXHIBIT 3–1 (*concluded*)

_____ Account number
_____ Social security number
_____ Date account was opened
_____ Other (Specify) _____
_____ Other (Specify) _____

KEY FEATURES

All portfolio management software packages operate in the same basic way. You enter key portfolio information, and the software performs a series of calculations and manipulates the data into a variety of standard report formats. Individual investors usually enter information for only one or two portfolios. On the other hand, a professional would enter information for numerous portfolios, one or more for each of his clients.

Regardless of whether you are professional, the capability to maintain multiple portfolios is important. You may want to track securities that you don't own but are considering purchasing. Or you may want to track different types of securities and compare their performance to your actual holdings. In these situations, it is best to maintain portfolios of holdings that you are interested in separate from your actual holdings. Likewise, professionals need the capability of multiple portfolios in order to keep track of each client's holdings.

SECURITY TYPES

Another key factor when evaluating portfolio management software packages is the type of securities that can be maintained in a portfolio. Professionally oriented packages can usually track a wide range of security types, including common stocks, preferred stocks, corporate bonds, municipal bonds, convertible bonds, mutual funds, money market funds, options, warrants, U.S. Treasury bonds and notes, commodities, futures, and other types of securities.

Packages for the individual investor tend to be more limited. In fact, some packages will enable you to track only stocks. Keep in mind the types of securities you currently own or plan to purchase when looking at the various packages.

DATA ENTRY

Entering data into a portfolio management software package is usually a straightforward process. For each portfolio and each security type, the program prompts you to enter information. For example, for each stock you own, you would typically enter the ticker symbol, company name, purchase date, number of shares purchased, total cost or cost per share, and whether you bought the stock in cash or on margin. Some packages will ask you to enter commissions separately to facilitate tracking your commission costs. Others lump the commissions in with the total cost or cost per share figure.

After entering your initial holdings, you will be asked for information each time you purchase or sell a security. For example, if you sell a stock, you will be prompted to enter the stock's ticker symbol, number of shares sold, sale date, and total sale price or sale price per share.

If you sell less than the total number of shares you own, you indicate which shares you sold. For example, assume that you bought 100 shares of XYZ Corporation for $80 per share in July 1978 and another 100 shares of XYZ Corporation for $140 in September 1986. In December 1986, you decide to sell 100 shares at a price of $120 per share. Most portfolio management software packages have the capability to match the 100 shares you sell with either the ones you bought in July 1978 or September 1986. This is important in determining whether there is a gain or loss on the sale and whether it is short- or long-term as defined by the Internal Revenue Service.

In this example, if you match the 100 shares sold with those purchased in July 1978, you will have a long-term gain of $4,000. If, on the other hand, you match the 100 shares sold with those purchased in September 1986, you will have a short-term loss of $2,000. The effect of matching sales with prior purchases can have a significant effect on your income taxes.

Updating your portfolio with current prices can be accomplished manually or automatically from an on-line service, such as the Dow Jones News/Retrieval. If you have a limited number of securities, you may choose to manually enter current security prices for each of your holdings. However, most portfolio management software packages have the capability to retrieve current prices from an on-line service. If you have more than a few securities to price out, automatically updating current prices will save you time and reduce the chance of data entry errors.

REPORTS

Reports are the most important part of a portfolio management software package. They enable you to look at your holdings from a number of different perspectives.

For most of the packages geared toward individuals, report formats are predefined and cannot be changed; packages for professionals often allow you to create custom reports.

The most common type of report reflects a portfolio's current status. It normally lists each security by name and indicates the type of security, whether it was purchased in cash or on margin, the number of shares or units owned, purchase price, current price, and gain or loss in both dollars and percent. Also, the total unrealized gain or loss is frequently presented and divided into short- and long-term components. If you have more than one portfolio, a separate report can be prepared for each portfolio.

A second report contains vital income tax information. A tax year profit/loss statement lists each security you sold during the tax year, specifying the number of shares, purchase date, sale date, total cost, total proceeds, and short- and long-term gain or loss. This report contains all the information needed to complete Schedule D of your federal income tax return.

If you want to examine information on only one security, most packages will generate an individual security report. This report includes many elements of a portfolio's current status report— the purchase date, whether the security was purchased in cash or on margin, number of shares, purchase price per share, total purchase cost, current price per share, total current value, gain or loss per share, total gain or loss, commissions paid when purchased, and dividends received to date. In addition, if an option has been written on a stock, the report shows relevant option information.

Two reports available with some software reflect current income from interest and dividends. The interest income report typically gives the interest earned on bonds, money market funds, certificates of deposit, and bank accounts. The dividend income report usually shows the dividends paid for each stock along with the dates they were paid. Both reports are prepared on a calendar year basis and are useful for determining income tax liabilities.

Other common reports will alert you to upcoming events. For example, many portfolio management software packages can identify securities that will go long-term as defined by the Internal Revenue Service in a given number of days (i.e., 30 days). Such reports help you adjust your investment strategy to meet your current tax position.

Another report will identify dividends and interest due in the near future, such as the next 30 days, to help you manage your cash flow better.

Additional reports are unique to professionally oriented packages. A security cross-reference list allows professionals to screen through portfolio data and list all clients that own a specific security. This helps professionals quickly identify which clients might be affected by a particular news event. For example, assume a broker hears a rumor that XYZ Corporation might be bought out by another company. He can quickly list the clients owning stock in XYZ Corporation along with how many shares each owns to determine the potential effect on his clients.

PROFESSIONAL CAPABILITIES

Professional portfolio management software packages have a number of unique capabilities that not only track client investments but also help professionals prospect for new clients.

The professional packages have more extensive database capabilities than packages designed for individuals. In addition to entering information on clients' securities, professionals can enter data on clients' and prospective clients' interests, occupations, investment preferences, and other characteristics. Later, this information can be screened to identify clients meeting specified criteria, such as those interested in municipal bonds or high-technology stocks. After screening the data, the package can often be instructed to generate a list of names, addresses, account numbers, and phone numbers. Alternatively, a set of mailing labels can be printed, and personalized client and prospect letters can be prepared based on security holdings and interest criteria.

Another important characteristic of packages for professionals is the capability to maintain extensive notes on telephone conversations with clients and prospects. Because professionals regularly talk to many clients and prospects, it is important for them to keep track of what is said to whom and when.

Many professional packages have a calendar feature that allows users to leave reminders to follow up a conversation on a specific date. Periodically, usually on a daily or weekly basis, the user can print out these reminders and take the appropriate action.

USING A TYPICAL PORTFOLIO MANAGEMENT SOFTWARE PACKAGE

To illustrate the benefits of a portfolio management software package, let's examine a typical one, Stock Portfolio System from Smith Micro Software, Inc. Stock Portfolio System is designed for the individual investor. Exhibit 3–2 provides a completed port-folio management software questionnaire for the IBM PC version. Remember, the purpose of the questionnaire is to help you ensure that the software has all of the features you require before you buy it.

Most software packages require you to perform a series of steps, known as installation procedures, before you actually use the software. These procedures are done only once, the first time you use the software on your personal computer. They normally take only a few minutes and involve such things as transferring the disk operating system to the software disk and installing the software on a hard disk drive if you have one.

It is also prudent to make one or more backup copies of the software disk at this time. These should be put away for safe keeping in the event something happens to the original software disk. If the software is copy protected, you won't be able to make a backup copy. In this case, the vendor usually provides two sets of disks, one original and one backup.

Stock Portfolio System is copy protected. Each user receives a free backup copy when Smith Micro Software, Inc., receives a completed license agreement/registration form from the user.

The installation procedures for Stock Portfolio Systems are easy—in fact, there are none if you do not have a hard disk drive.

To start the IBM PC version of Stock Portfolio System, you must first load the disk operating system (DOS). Next, you simply type "SPS" and press the Enter key. At that time, the program's Main Menu appears on the screen.

EXHIBIT 3–2   Completed Portfolio Management Software Questionnaire for Stock Portfolio System—IBM PC Version

---

GENERAL INFORMATION

Product name: Stock Portfolio System   Version #: 3rd Ed.

Vendor name: Smith Micro Software, Inc.

Address: P.O. Box 7137

                 Huntington Beach, CA 92615

Telephone: (714) 964–0412

List price: $225.00

Demonstration diskette available?   _____ Yes   _X_ No

    If yes, what is the price of the demonstration diskette? _____N/A*_____

Money-back guarantee available?   _____ Yes   _X_ No

    If yes, how many days?   _N/A_

HARDWARE REQUIREMENTS

Operating system: _X_ DOS 1.1 or later   _____Other (Specify) _____

                  _____ DOS 2.0 or later

Minimum memory required: ___ 64K   ___ 128K _X_ 192K ___ 256K

Number of disk drives required: _____ 1 single-sided

                                _____ 2 single-sided

                                _X_ 1 double-sided

                                _____ 2 double-sided

                                Other _____

Color graphics required?   _____ Yes   _X_ No

Modem required?   _____ Yes   _X_ No

Modem recommended?   _X_ Yes   _____ No

Printer required?   _____ Yes   _X_ No

Printer recommended? _X_ Yes   _____ No

Other hardware requirements (specify): None _____

_____

_____

PRODUCT SUPPORT

Who provides support for the product? Smith Micro Software, Inc.

Is there a telephone number available for support?   _X_ Yes   _____ No

    If yes, is it toll-free?   _____ Yes   _X_ No

    Days of the week support is available: Monday to Friday

    Hours of the day support is available: 9 AM to 5 PM Pacific time

Is the software copy protected?   _X_ Yes   _____ No

    If yes, can you copy program to a hard disk?   _X_ Yes   _____ No

    Cost of backup copy? The user receives a free backup copy when Smith

---

EXHIBIT 3–2 *(continued)*

Micro Software, Inc. receives his completed license agreement/registration form.
Defective disk replacement policy: <u>Defective disk will be replaced at no charge</u>
<u>for a period of 90 days after the date of original purchase.</u>

Update policy: <u>All registered users are notified of system upgrades and provided</u>
<u>with an upgrade offer. The cost of the most recent upgrade was $40.</u>
<u>Additionally, users can pay a $65 annual fee that automatically entitles the</u>
<u>user to all upgrades during the year.</u>

DOCUMENTATION

Number of pages in user's manual? ___84___

User's manual includes:

	Yes	No
Tutorial	X	
Index		X
Glossary		X
Explanation of error messages		X
Sample applications	X	
Samples of screen displays	X	
Samples of printed output	X	

Does the package include a tutorial on disk? ____ Yes _X_ No
Does the package include a reference card? ____ Yes _X_ No
Does the disk contain sample applications? ____ Yes _X_ No
　　If yes, how many and what type? _N/A_____
Does the package include a demonstration disk? ____ Yes _X_ No

EASE OF USE

Estimated time to learn basic functions:
　_X_ Less than 1 day ____ 1 to 6 days ____ 1 to 2 weeks
　____ Over 2 weeks

Commands are abbreviated for quick entry? _X_ Yes ____ No
Error messages are provided on screen? _X_ Yes ____ No
Programs are menu driven? _X_ Yes ____ No
Help screens are available? ____ At all times
　　　　　　　　　　　　　____ At various points in the program
　　　　　　　　　　　　　_X_ Nonexistent
How experienced with the IBM PC should a person be to use this package?
　____ Very ____ Somewhat _X_ Little ____ No experience

SECURITY TYPES

Which of the following types of securities can be maintained in a portfolio?
　(Check all that apply)
　_X_ Common Stocks　　　　_X_ Options
　_X_ Preferred stocks　　　　_X_ Warrants
　_X_ Corporate bonds　　　　_X_ Commodities

EXHIBIT 3–2 *(continued)*

__X__ Municipal bonds   __X__ Futures
__X__ U.S. Treasury   __X__ Other (Specify) _____ Money markets
     bonds and notes
__X__ Convertible bonds   __X__ Other (Specify) Certificates of deposit
__X__ Mutual funds

DATA ENTRY

Is the user prompted for data to be entered?   __X__ Yes   _____ No
Which of the following items are entered? (Check all that apply)
__X__ Security symbol   __X__ Purchase price or sell value
                                              (per share or total)
__X__ Security description   _____ Ex-dividend date
__X__ Security classification   __X__ Dividend rate
__X__ Transaction date   __X__ Yield
__X__ Quantity bought   __X__ Margined positions
__X__ Quantity sold   __X__ Margin interest rate
__X__ Commission   __X__ Current market price per unit
_____ Other (Specify) _____
_____ Other (Specify) _____
Can the user access an on-line database for current price updates?
__X__ Yes   _____ No
If yes, which on-line database is accessed? (Check all that apply)
__X__ Dow Jones News/Retrieval
_____ Warner Computer Systems
_____ Other (Specify) _____
_____ Other (Specify) _____
Does the software allow for entry of fractional prices?   _____ Yes   __X__ No
Does the software allow for entry of the maturity date of bonds?
__X__ Yes   _____ No
Does the software allow for the entry of option expiration dates?
__X__ Yes   _____ No
Can the user record short sales?   __X__ Yes   _____ No
Can the user record the writing of covered calls and puts?
__X__ Yes   _____ No
Can the user record margined positions?   __X__ Yes   _____ No
After data is entered, can it be easily checked and changed?
__X__ Yes   _____ No

FEATURES

What is the maximum number of portfolios per disk? No limit _____
What is the maximum number of securities per portfolio? 150 _____
What is the maximum number of transactions per security? No limit _____
Can the user classify securities into fixed categories?
_____ Yes   __X__ No
Can the user classify securities into user-definable categories?
_____ Yes   __X__ No

EXHIBIT 3–2 (*continued*)

Can items be cross-referenced between portfolios? _____ Yes __X__ No
If yes, which of the following items can be cross-referenced? (Check all
that apply) N/A
_____ Security symbol
_____ Number of shares
_____ Purchase price
_____ Percentage gain or loss
_____ Other (Specify) _____
_____ Other (Specify) _____
Can securities be sorted by type? _____ Yes __X__ No
Can securities be sorted alphabetically? __X__ Yes _____ No
Can securities be sorted by date of purchase? _____ Yes __X__ No
Are sells matched with previous buys? __X__ Yes _____ No
Is the update of one security in one portfolio transferred to all
portfolios? _____ Yes __X__ No

REPORTS

Can reports be generated on the screen? __X__ Yes _____ No
Can reports be printed? __X__ Yes _____ No
Which of the following types of reports can be generated? (Check all that apply)
__X__ Current portfolio status report
__X__ Cash portfolio status report
__X__ Dividend/bond interest due report
__X__ Dividend income report
__X__ Individual security status report
__X__ Long-term status report
__X__ Interest income report
__X__ Tax year profit/loss report
__X__ Other (Specify) Transaction Audit Lists _____
Which of the following items do reports display? (Check all that apply)
__X__ Security description
__X__ Purchase date
__X__ Quantity purchased
__X__ Latest market price per unit
__X__ Current value of each security
__X__ Total current value of portfolio
__X__ Unrealized gains and losses
__X__ Stock position—long or short
__X__ Holdings about to go long-term
_____ Holdings nearing user-defined high-price limits
_____ Holdings nearing user-defined low-price limits
__X__ Commissions and fees paid when security purchased
_____ Calculated commissions to be paid when position is closed

---

EXHIBIT 3–2 (*concluded*)

__X__ Dividends received per security
__X__ Percentage yield on purchase cost
_____ Percentage yield on current value
_____ Percentage of each security to the total portfolio
__X__ Short-term gain or loss per transaction
__X__ Long-term gain or loss per transaction
_____ Other (Specify) _____
_____ Other (Specify) _____

CLIENT INFORMATION (Complete this section only if software is intended to be used by professionals to manage client portfolios.)
Which of the following items are maintained for each client? (Check all that apply)   N/A
_____ Name
_____ Address
_____ Telephone number
_____ Account number
_____ Social security number
_____ Date account was opened
_____ Other (Specify) _____
_____ Other (Specify) _____

---

*N/A = Not applicable.

As illustrated in Exhibit 3–3, the Main Menu gives you six choices: Portfolio Utilities, Update Portfolio, Generate Reports and Status, Dow Jones News and Quotes, System Parameters, and Terminate Run.

Setting System Parameters

Choice five, System Parameters, will define the limits of your system. By defining the system parameters (as illustrated in Exhibit 3–4), your personal computer will know which disk drive to read program and portfolio files from, the type of monitor (monochrome or color) you are using, and if you are using a printer and/or modem. Modem users also indicate the speed of transmission, 300 or 1200 baud, a Dow Jones News/Retrieval password, the communications network to be used, the telephone number, and type of telephone. In addition, the program allows you to enter a fiscal year different from the calendar year, an estimated

EXHIBIT 3-3 Stock Portfolio System's Main Menu Structure

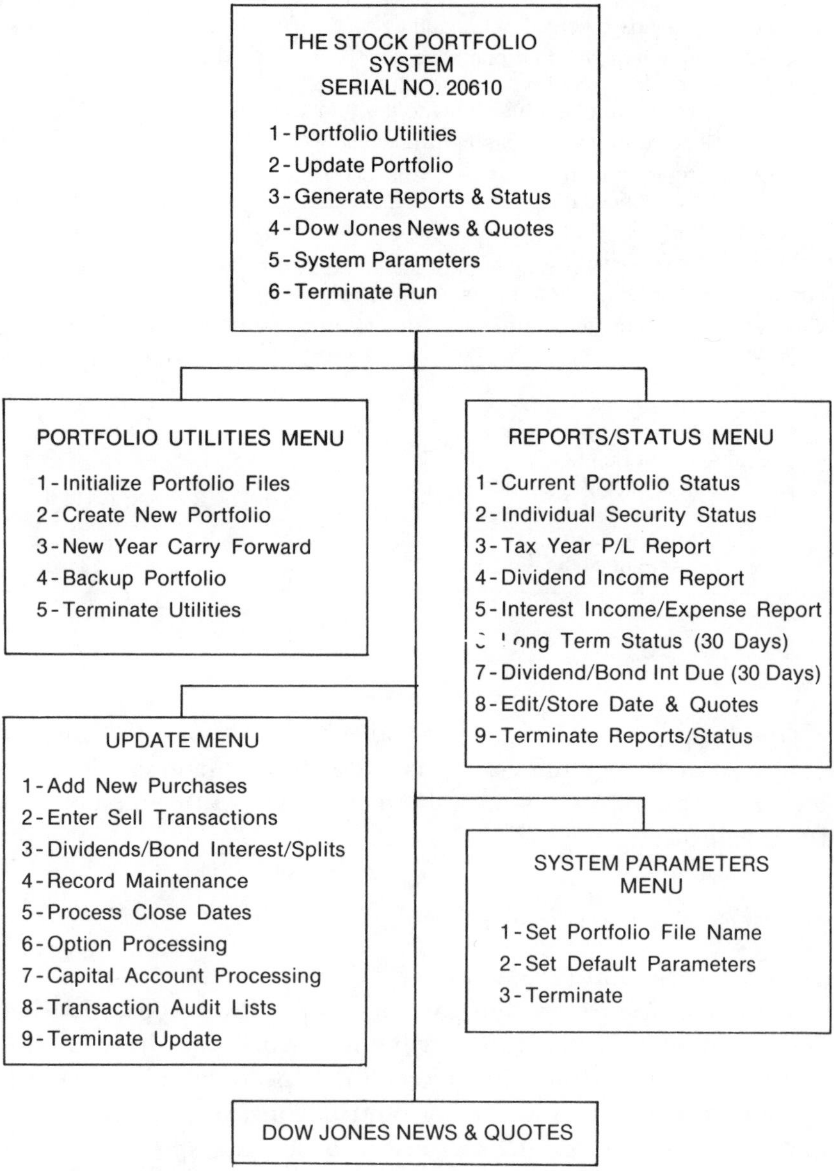

THE STOCK PORTFOLIO
SYSTEM
SERIAL NO. 20610

1 - Portfolio Utilities
2 - Update Portfolio
3 - Generate Reports & Status
4 - Dow Jones News & Quotes
5 - System Parameters
6 - Terminate Run

PORTFOLIO UTILITIES MENU

1 - Initialize Portfolio Files
2 - Create New Portfolio
3 - New Year Carry Forward
4 - Backup Portfolio
5 - Terminate Utilities

REPORTS/STATUS MENU

1 - Current Portfolio Status
2 - Individual Security Status
3 - Tax Year P/L Report
4 - Dividend Income Report
5 - Interest Income/Expense Report
6 - Long Term Status (30 Days)
7 - Dividend/Bond Int Due (30 Days)
8 - Edit/Store Date & Quotes
9 - Terminate Reports/Status

UPDATE MENU

1 - Add New Purchases
2 - Enter Sell Transactions
3 - Dividends/Bond Interest/Splits
4 - Record Maintenance
5 - Process Close Dates
6 - Option Processing
7 - Capital Account Processing
8 - Transaction Audit Lists
9 - Terminate Update

SYSTEM PARAMETERS
MENU

1 - Set Portfolio File Name
2 - Set Default Parameters
3 - Terminate

DOW JONES NEWS & QUOTES

EXHIBIT 3–4 System Parameters

```
                    SYSTEM PARAMETERS

Disk on which SPS Resident . . . . . . . . A
Disk on which Portfolio Resident . . . . . B
Monitor Type, Mono = 1, Color = 2 . . . . 1

Fiscal Year Accounting(Y OR N) . . . . . . N
       Fiscal Year Begins(01=JAN, 12=DEC) . 00
Estimated Tax Rate % . . . . . . . . . . . 30
Margin Purchase Requirements for
       Account#1 /Stocks/Options/Bonds/ . . 50
       Account#2 /Bonds/ . . . . . . . . . . 30
       Account#3 /Bonds/ . . . . . . . . . . 25

Printer Name or 'N' for none . . . . . . . LPT1
Hayes Modem, 'N'=none or 1=COM1, 2=COM2. . 1
Line Speed, 300 Baud = 1, 1200 Baud = 2 . 2
Dow Jones Password  . . . . . . . . . . . XXXXXXXXXX
Telenet = 1, Tymnet = 2, Uninet = 3 . . . 2
Phone #  . . . . . . . . . . . . . . . . . 452-1018
(R)otary or (T)ouch. . . . . . . . . . . . T


        UPDATE AS REQUIRED,   PRESS  <TAB> TO SKIP
```

tax rate, and a percentage for margin requirements. Once set, the system parameters can be easily changed.

Using Portfolio Utilities

Selecting choice two from the Main Menu leads you to the Portfolio Utilities Menu. The first choice on the Portfolio Utilities Menu, initialize portfolio files, lets you get a blank disk ready to record portfolio information. The second choice, create new portfolio, is used to record key portfolio information on the securities you own when you first use Stock Portfolio System.

A third utility, new year carry forward, is used at the end of each year. In essence, this utility creates a new portfolio for the coming year. It copies active securities from the old portfolio to the new one.

The final utility is used to make a backup copy of portfolio files to prevent accidental loss.

Updating Your Portfolio

Selecting choice two from the Main Menu leads you to the Update Menu. The Update Menu allows you to add new purchases, enter sell transactions, and record dividends, interest on bonds, and stock splits. In addition, you can edit previously entered data in the event of an error.

Entering purchases or sales information is straightforward. For each new purchase, the system asks for the ticker symbol, company name, purchase date, close date, purchase type (cash, margin, bond, or mutual fund), number of shares, price per share, and purchase commission. If it is a short sale, you simply enter a negative number for the number of shares purchased.

For each sell transaction, you enter the ticker symbol, sale date, number of shares sold, price per share, and commission. If you are selling only part of your shares, you also specify which shares you are selling. For example, suppose you own 200 shares of XYZ Corporation, 100 purchased in August 1975 and 100 in July 1985. When you sell 100 shares of the stock, you will need to match the sale with one of the two purchases.

The Update Menu also enables you to generate a Transaction Audit List. It lists key information by date for each transaction, such as the purchase or sale of a stock, giving you a quick way to double-check the information used to update your portfolio.

Generating Reports

Selecting choice three from the Main Menu leads you to the Reports/Status Menu. This is the section of the program that you will use the most to generate reports on an ongoing basis. The reports are the key part of a portfolio management software package. They tell you how much your securities are worth and how your investments are doing.

Before generating reports, you normally enter new quotes for each of your securities. This can be done manually, but more often prices are automatically retrieved from an on-line service, such as Dow Jones News/Retrieval.

Once you have updated the security prices, Stock Portfolio System allows you to generate reports similar to those of most portfolio management software packages. (See Exhibits 3–5 through 3–11.) Items included in each report follows.

Report Name	Exhibit Number	Items Included in Report
Current Portfolio Status	3–5	1. Purchase type: C-Cash; M-Margin; O-Option; B-Bond; or F-Mutual Fund 2. Investment term: Short-term or long-term 3. Security name 4. Number of shares 5. Purchase price per share 6. Current price per share 7. Gain or loss per share 8. Percent change 9. Account percentage requirement: the margin maintenance requirement 10. Margin account equity: current equity in your margin account 11. Account percent equity 12. Purchasing power: the total dollars available for margin investing that will maintain equity requirements 13. Portfolio purchase value 14. Portfolio current value 15. Total unrealized gain or loss 16. Total unrealized short-term gain or loss 17. Total unrealized long-term gain or loss 18. Commission data
Individual Security Status	3–6	1. Purchase date 2. Close date 3. Number of shares 4. Purchase type 5. Purchase price per share 6. Total purchase price 7. Current price per share 8. Total current price 9. Gain or loss per share 10. Total gain or loss 11. Purchase commission 12. Sell commission, if applicable 13. Dividends received to date 14. Total gain or loss after dividends and commissions 15. Option data 16. Percent return on investment 17. After tax gain or loss 18. Percent after tax return on investment

Report Name	Exhibit Number	Items Included in Report
Profit/Loss Statement	3–7	1. Security name 2. Number of shares 3. Purchase date 4. Total purchase cost 5. Sell date 6. Proceeds from sale 7. Short-term gain or loss 8. Long-term gain or loss 9. Net gain or loss
Dividend Income Statement	3–8	1. Stock name 2. Date paid 3. Dividend paid: ordinary income, tax free, or capital gain 4. Total dividend income
Interest Income/ Expense Statement	3–9	1. Interest income by month 2. Total interest income 3. Interest expense by month 4. Total interest expense
Long-Term Status	3–10	1. Security name 2. Purchase date 3. Total purchase cost 4. Total current value 5. Gain or loss 6. Total gain or loss
Dividends/Bonds Interest Due	3–11	1. Number of shares 2. Security name 3. Frequency dividends paid 4. Last date paid 5. Last total amount paid 6. Total dividends due

---

EXHIBIT 3–5 Sample Current Portfolio Status Report

```
                    CURRENT PORTFOLIO STATUS
                      FOR JOE INVESTOR
                      AS OF 12/26/85

PURCH INVEST   SECURITY      NO. OF PURCHASE  CURRENT  GAIN/LOSS PERCENT
 TYPE  TERM      NAME         SHARES PRICE/SHR PRICE/SHR PER SHR  CHANGE
----------------------------------------------------------------------

  C   LONG   APPLE COMPUTER      100   51.25    21.75    -29.50   -57%
  M   SHORT  COMPAQ COMPUTER     250   10.38    12.75      2.38    22%
  C   LONG  *INT'L BUSINESS MACH 100   60.00   153.25     93.25   155%
  B   SHORT  PAC T&T 8.65% 2005    5   77.50    85.50      8.00    10%


--------------------------MARGIN ACCOUNT DATA------------------------
       ACCOUNT % REQ     EQUITY $    % EQUITY    PURCHASING POWER
           50            1920.10      72.38          1187.50
           30               0.00       0.00             0.00
           25               0.00       0.00             0.00

-----------------------------SUMMARY DATA---------------------------
       PORTFOLIO PURCHASE VALUE             17,593.75
       PORTFOLIO CURRENT VALUE              24,962.50
       TOTAL UNREALIZED GAIN/LOSS            7,368.75
                                           ==========
       TOTAL UNREALIZED SHORT TERM GAIN/LOSS   993.75
       TOTAL UNREALIZED LONG TERM GAIN/LOSS   6,375.00
                                           ==========
       PURCHASE COMMISSIONS                    480.56
       SALES COMMISSIONS AND COSTS             203.58
                                           ----------
       TOTAL COMMISSIONS & COSTS YEAR-TO-DATE  684.14
                                           ==========
```

EXHIBIT 3–6 Sample Individual Security Status Report

```
                  IBM STOCK REPORT
                   AS OF 12/26/85
PUR DATE    06/06/82  CLOSE DATE    06/13/82

# OF SHRS        100  PURCHASE TYPE       C

PURCH $/SHR    60.00  TOT PUR $      6000.00

CURR $/SHR    153.25  TOT CURR $    15325.00

G/L / SHR      93.25  GAIN/LOSS      9325.00

PURCH COST     80.00  SELL COST         0.00

DIVIDENDS    1460.00  TOTAL G/L     10705.00
----------------OPTION WRITTEN----------------
EXPIR DAT  01/17/86  GAIN-OPT.       391.00

OPT. $/SH    155.00  G/L IF EX      9811.00
RET ON INV     177%  AFT TAX G/L    7493.50

AFT TAX ROI    124%
```

EXHIBIT 3–7 Sample Profit/Loss Statement

```
NAME:  JOE INVESTOR        TAX ID#:  123-45-6789


                       PROFIT/LOSS STATEMENT
                            FOR 1985
                         AS OF 12/26/85

                   # OF   PURCH DATE  TOTAL COST   G A I N / L O S S
       SECURITY NAME   SHARES  SELL DATE   PROCEEDS     SHORT       LONG
-----------------------------------------------------------------------

INT'L BUSINESS MACH     100   06/06/82    6,189.28
                              12/19/85   15,425.00      0.00     9,235.72
LOTUS DEVELOPMENT       100   07/26/85    2,996.55
                              12/20/85    2,550.00   -446.55        0.00
                                                    ---------   ---------
                                   NET GAIN/LOSS    -446.55     9,235.72


        NET PROFIT/LOSS(SHORT + LONG) FOR 1985      8,789.17
```

EXHIBIT 3–8 Sample Dividend Income Statement

```
NAME:  JOE INVESTOR          SS#:  123-45-6789


                     DIVIDEND INCOME STATEMENT
                            FOR 1985
                         AS OF 12/26/85

              STOCK NAME     DATE PAID   ORD INC  TAX FREE  CAP GAIN
       -----------------------------------------------------------------

       INT'L BUSINESS MACH   03/13/85    220.00     0.00      0.00
       INT'L BUSINESS MACH   06/12/85    220.00     0.00      0.00
       INT'L BUSINESS MACH   09/11/85    220.00     0.00      0.00
       INT'L BUSINESS MACH   12/18/85    220.00     0.00      0.00
                                        --------  --------  --------
       TOTAL DIVIDEND INCOME             880.00     0.00      0.00
                                        ========  ========  ========
```

EXHIBIT 3–9   Sample Interest Income/
Expense Statement

```
INTEREST INCOME/EXPENSE STATEMENT
              FOR 1985
          AS OF 12/26/85

MONTH             INCOME         EXPENSE
-------------------------------------------
  JAN             730.06          25.80
  FEB             525.00          26.50
  MAR              26.88          29.00
  APR             744.27          35.00
  MAY              50.00          26.77
  JUNE            557.90          24.15
  JULY            765.53          31.80
  AUG              48.73          27.98
  SEPT            413.12          23.10
  OCT              75.00          35.60
  NOV             618.85          31.00
  DEC               0.00           0.00
                 ---------       ---------
ANNUAL TOTAL     4555.37         316.70
```

EXHIBIT 3–10   Sample Long-Term Status Report

```
            SECURITIES GOING LONG TERM
                 IN NEXT 30 DAYS
                 AS OF 12/26/85

  SECURITY          PURCHASE    PURCHASE    CURRENT    GAIN/
  NAME              DATE        COST        VALUE      LOSS
-----------------------------------------------------------------

COMPAQ COMPUTER     07/09/85    2593.75     3187.50      593.75
                                                       ----------
                                            TOTAL G/L    593.75
```

EXHIBIT 3–11   Sample Dividends/Bonds Interest Due Report

```
            DIVIDENDS/BOND INTEREST DUE
                 IN NEXT 30 DAYS
                 AS OF 11/26/85

# OF                          DIVIDEND    LAST DATE    LAST TOTAL
SHARES     SECURITY NAME      PAID        PAID         AMOUNT PAID
-----------------------------------------------------------------

 200       INT'L BUS MACHINE  QUARTERLY   09/11/85       220.00
                                                        --------
                                   TOTAL DIVIDENDS DUE   220.00
```

Dow Jones News and Quotes

A common feature among portfolio management software packages is the capability to access an on-line service to retrieve information other than just current quotes. Stock Portfolio System is no exception.

Using Stock Portfolio System you can access the Dow Jones News/Retrieval for company and industry news, current earnings estimates, historical quotes, company financial statements, and a variety of other financial information.

OTHER PORTFOLIO MANAGEMENT SOFTWARE PACKAGES

Although other portfolio management software packages have different features and capabilities, the majority operate like Stock Portfolio System. The number of portfolio management software packages available changes constantly. New software is coming to market, while other packages are dropping out. To obtain a complete up-to-date listing of portfolio management software packages, get the latest copy of *The Individual Investors Microcomputer Resource Guide* from the American Association of Individual Investors (see Appendix A).

CHAPTER 4

The Spreadsheet Alternative

Many investors use spreadsheet programs, such as Lotus 1-2-3, as an alternative to purchasing portfolio management software packages. These investors have found that spreadsheet programs are readily available and relatively easy to use. They also offer the user a great deal of flexibility in setting up electronic worksheets that meet their individual investment needs.

By using one of the popular spreadsheet programs, investors can overcome several disadvantages associated with typical portfolio management software packages. One of the main drawbacks to using a typical portfolio management software package is that reports are predefined and set up in a format that cannot be changed. Often, you do not have the flexibility to add to or delete from the information presented in reports or to create additional reports.

Using a spreadsheet program, this limitation can be overcome. Spreadsheet templates, the phrase used to describe electronic worksheets, can be constructed to present information in virtually any format that is suitable for your individual needs. For example, if you have been maintaining worksheets of your portfolio information by hand, you may wish to create identical worksheets using a spreadsheet program that takes advantage of the computer's speed and accuracy.

A second deterrent to the use of portfolio management software packages is the difficulty of locating a package that meets an investor's individual needs. Because of the specialized nature of the software, local computer stores do not normally sell the packages and are not equipped with personnel who can provide you with the information you need to make a purchasing decision.

Individuals unable to locate a package meeting their needs often turn to spreadsheet programs as a logical second choice.

A final roadblock is cost. Many individuals simply do not want to pay the price for the software given the size of their portfolios. Often, these same individuals own or have access to a spreadsheet program that can adequately serve their needs.

On the other hand, using a spreadsheet program to monitor a portfolio is not for everyone. It does require that you own or have access to a spreadsheet program and that you are spreadsheet literate, that is, that you know how to use the various features of a spreadsheet program to construct an electronic worksheet.

In addition, one of the main attractions of a typical portfolio management software package is the ability to retrieve current security prices from an on-line service, such as the Dow Jones News/Retrieval, and automatically price out your portfolio. Using a spreadsheet program by itself will not enable you to do this. However, as you will see later, using a spreadsheet link program in conjunction with a spreadsheet program will facilitate automatic retrieval of current security prices and updating of a portfolio.

CONSTRUCTING A SPREADSHEET TEMPLATE

Before constructing a spreadsheet template to monitor your portfolio, first decide what information you want to include. Do you want to include only stocks? Or do you want to include other types of investments, such as bonds, options, mutual funds, and commodities? What about cash and real estate?

The value of a spreadsheet program is that you have the flexibility to control the information that is included. You can construct a spreadsheet template that will present the information of the greatest benefit to you in making investment decisions. And, as time goes on, you can easily change the template to reflect changes in your portfolio of investments.

Next, define the items you want included for each security or other type of investment and, more importantly, the measures of performance you want to use. Exhibit 4–1 shows a spreadsheet template that has been constructed to monitor a portfolio of stocks using Lotus 1-2-3. For those interested in constructing a similar template, the formulas and column widths used have been noted on the exhibit.

EXHIBIT 4–1 Spreadsheet Template That Can Be Used to Monitor a Portfolio of Stocks

```
 ! A !    B     !  C  ! D ! E ! F  !  G  !  H  !  I  !  J  !  K ! L  !  M  !  N  !
1!
2!
3! ===============================================================================================
4!                                          COLUMN WIDTHS
5! ---------------------------------------------------------------------------------------------
6!    6      18        10    6   8   9     10     9     9     9     7    8      9     9
7! ===============================================================================================
8!
9!
10!                                        J.P. INVESTOR
11!
12!                                   PORTFOLIO STATUS REPORT
13!
14!                                          24-Jan-86
15!
16!
17! ---------------------------------------------------------------------------------------------
18!                                                           UNREALIZED
19!                                                           GAIN/LOSS
20!                               NUMBER  COST           CURRENT      ----------------PERCENT      YIELD  YIELD ON
21! TICKER                           OF   PER    TOTAL  PRICE PER CURRENT  SHORT- LONG- GAIN/ ANNUAL   ON   CURRENT
22! SYMBOL  COMPANY NAME      DATE  SHARES SHARE  COST    SHARE    VALUE    TERM   TERM  LOSS DIVIDEND COST   VALUE
23! ---------------------------------------------------------------------------------------------
24! GE    General Electric 14-Mar-77 100  25.13 2512.50   68.88  6887.50   0.00 4375.00  174% 2.20    8.76%  3.19%
25! IBM   Int'l Bus. Mach. 06-Jun-82 100  60.00 6000.00  150.88 15087.50   0.00 9087.50  151% 4.40    7.33%  2.92%
26! PEP   Pepsico          14-Mar-84 100  37.25 3725.00   69.88  6987.50   0.00 3262.50   88% 1.78    4.78%  2.55%
27! LOTS  Lotus Dev. Corp. 26-Jul-85 200  28.75 5750.00   25.00  5000.00   0.00 -750.00  -13% 0.00    0.00%  0.00%
28! CMPQ  Compaq Computer  09-Aug-85 200  10.38 2075.00   13.25  2650.00 575.00    0.00   28% 0.00    0.00%  0.00%
29! ...   ................ .......... ...  ..... ........ ...... ........ ...... ........ .... ....    .....  .....
30! ...   ................ .......... ...  ..... ........ ...... ........ ...... ........ .... ....    .....  .....
31! ...   ................ .......... ...  ..... ........ ...... ........ ...... ........ .... ....    .....  .....
32! ...   ................ .......... ...  ..... ........ ...... ........ ...... ........ .... ....    .....  .....
33! ...   ................ .......... ...  ..... ........ ...... ........ ...... ........ .... ....    .....  .....
34! ---------------------------------------------------------------------------------------------
35!
36! TOTALS:                             20062.50        36612.50 575.00 15975.00   82%
37! ===============================================================================================
38!
39! ENTER DATES AS @DATE(YY,MM,DD)
40!
41! FORMULAS OF CELLS IN ROW 24...            FORMULAS OF CELLS IN ROW 36...
42!
43!    F24   +D24*E24                         F36   @SUM(F24.F33)
44!
45!    H24   +D24*G24                         H36   @SUM(H24.H33)
46!
47!    I24   @IF((G14-C24)>180,0,H24-F24)     I36   @SUM(I24.I33)
48!
49!    J24   @IF((G14-C24)>180,H24-F24,0)     J36   @SUM(J24.J33)
50!
51!    K24   @IF((G14-C24)>180,J24/F24,I24/F24)  K36  (I36+J36)/F36
52!
53!    M24   +L24/E24
54!
55!    N24   +L24/G24
56!
57!
58!
59!
```

Let's examine how you would use this template. The first time you use the template, you enter the ticker symbol, company name, date of purchase, number of shares purchased, cost per share, current price per share, and annual dividend for each stock.

The template is set up to automatically calculate the total cost and current value of the portfolio. In addition, four measures of the portfolio's performance are calculated, namely the unrealized short- or long-term gain or loss, percent gain or loss, yield on cost, and yield on current value.

Any stock owned over 180 days is considered to be held long-term for income tax purposes and normally receives favorable tax treatment when compared to stocks held less than 180 days. To calculate the unrealized short- or long-term gain or loss on a stock, the template is set up to determine the number of days the stock has been held and then to classify the difference between the current value and total cost as either short- or long-term.

After you have entered information on the stocks you own, you can update your portfolio as frequently as you like. Updating requires only that you enter the current price per share for each stock and change the annual dividend, if required, for any of the stocks. Assuming you have a portfolio of 10 to 15 stocks, an update takes only a few minutes.

If you wish to maintain a permanent record for a given date, the column widths on the sample template have been set to facilitate printing of the template in a compressed mode on a standard 8½ × 11 sheet of paper.

SPREADSHEET LINK PROGRAMS

A spreadsheet link program enhances the value of using a spreadsheet program to monitor a portfolio of securities. Spreadsheet link programs facilitate the transfer of data, such as current price quotes, from an on-line database to your spreadsheet template.

The main advantage of a spreadsheet link program is that if you have more than a few securities, it makes updating the information in your portfolio faster. It also reduces the chance of typographical errors from entering data manually.

When you use a spreadsheet link program, you will incur charges for the actual time you are connected to an on-line database. These charges vary depending on the database and the time of access.

Let's take a closer look at two spreadsheet link programs, Dow Jones Spreadsheet Link™ and Market Link.

Dow Jones Spreadsheet Link

Dow Jones Spreadsheet Link from Dow Jones & Co., Inc., facilitates the transfer of financial information from the Dow Jones News/Retrieval to your spreadsheet template. You can automatically retrieve and store data, which can subsequently be combined with a spreadsheet template from several of the Dow Jones News/Retrieval databases, including Current Quotes, Historical Quotes, Media General Financial Services, Disclosure II, and Corporate Earnings Estimator. In addition, Dow Jones Spreadsheet Link includes a terminal program for access to all Dow Jones News/Retrieval databases and a program that uses data files from Dow Jones Market Manager Plus.™

You must construct your templates in a certain manner to use Dow Jones Spreadsheet Link. This construction does not limit your flexibility to perform calculations with the spreadsheet template; rather it enables Dow Jones News/Retrieval to recognize the specific information you are requesting.

In the first column of each template, you must enter the ticker symbols of the securities, preceded by the letter V and a hyphen (V-). For example, to retrieve information on IBM, you would enter V-IBM.

Across the top row of the template, you would also enter V-codes to identify the specific information you want to retrieve. For example, as illustrated in Exhibit 4–2, you would enter V-LAST at the top row of Column G to retrieve the current price per share. A complete list of V-codes is included in Exhibit 4–3.

The remainder of the template doesn't require any special instructions. You can include other rows and columns and perform calculations throughout the template. Once you complete designing the template, save it as you normally would. No special file name is required.

Next, you exit the spreadsheet program and load Dow Jones Spreadsheet Link. At the Main Menu, you choose retrieve information for the spreadsheet. When prompted, you enter the file name of the template you want to use.

At this point, Dow Jones Spreadsheet Link enters into an editing routine. During this edit, the program examines your tem-

---

EXHIBIT 4–2 Spreadsheet Template Constructed Using Dow Jones
Spreadsheet Link V-Codes

```
    ! A !     B     ! C !D ! E ! F ! G ! H ! I ! J ! K ! L ! M ! N !
 1!                                   V-LAST
 2!
 3!                              J.P. INVESTOR
 4!
 5!                          PORTFOLIO STATUS REPORT
 6!
 7!                               24-Jan-86
 8!
 9!
10! -----------------------------------------------------------------
11!                                                 UNREALIZED
12!                                                 GAIN/LOSS
13!                    NUMBER COST      CURRENT  ----------------PERCENT      YIELD YIELD ON
14! TICKER               OF   PER  TOTAL PRICE PER CURRENT SHORT- LONG- GAIN/ ANNUAL    ON   CURRENT
15! SYMBOL  COMPANY NAME  DATE  SHARES SHARE COST  SHARE  VALUE  TERM  TERM  LOSS DIVIDEND COST  VALUE
16! -----------------------------------------------------------------
17! V-GE   General Electric 14-Mar-77 100 25.13 2512.50        ERR  0.00  ERR  ERR  2.20  8.76%  ERR
18! V-IBM  Int'l Bus. Mach. 06-Jun-82 100 60.00 6000.00        ERR  0.00  ERR  ERR  4.40  7.33%  ERR
19! V-PEP  Pepsico         14-Mar-84 100 37.25 3725.00        ERR  0.00  ERR  ERR  1.78  4.78%  ERR
20! V-LOTS Lotus Dev. Corp. 26-Jul-85 200 28.75 5750.00        ERR  0.00  ERR  ERR  0.00  0.00%  ERR
21! V-CMPQ Compaq Computer  09-Aug-85 200 10.38 2075.00        ERR  ERR   0.00 ERR  0.00  0.00%  ERR
22! ...   ................ .......... ...  .....  ......  ......  ......  ......  ......  ....  ....  ...... .....
23! ...   ................ .......... ...  .....  ......  ......  ......  ......  ......  ....  ....  ...... .....
24! ...   ................ .......... ...  .....  ......  ......  ......  ......  ......  ....  ....  ...... .....
25! ...   ................ .......... ...  .....  ......  ......  ......  ......  ......  ....  ....  ...... .....
26! ...   ................ .......... ...  .....  ......  ......  ......  ......  ......  ....  ....  ...... .....
27! -----------------------------------------------------------------
28!
29! TOTALS:                          20062.50        ERR     ERR   ERR  ERR
30! =================================================================
31!
32!
33!
```

EXHIBIT 4–3 Information That Can Be Retrieved from Dow Jones News/
Retrieval for Use with a Spreadsheet Program

---

*Data Item
Identifier*   *Information*

CURRENT QUOTES DATABASE:

Data Item Identifier	Information
V-VOLUME	Current Day Volume
V-LAST	Latest Trade Price*
V-LOW	Current Day Low*
V-HIGH	Current Day High
V-OPEN	Current Day Open
V-CLOSE	Previous Day Close*
V-BID	Current Bid**
V-ASKED	Current Ask Price**
V-USBID	Current Bid***
V-USASK	Current Ask Price***
V-USYIELD	Annual Yield***

HISTORICAL QUOTES DATABASE:

V-VOLUME-MM/DD/YY	Volume on MM/DD/YY
V-CLOSE-MM/DD/YY	Close on MM/DD/YY*

EXHIBIT 4–3 (*continued*)

V-LOW-MM/DD/YY	Low trade on MM/DD/YY*
V-HIGH-MM/DD/YY	High trade on MM/DD/YY*
V-BID-MM/DD/YY	Last bid on MM/DD/YY**
V-ASKED-MM/DD/YY	Last ask on MM/DD/YY**

MEDIA GENERAL FINANCIAL SERVICES:

V-REV12	Revenue for last 12 months (millions)
V-REVFY	Revenue for last fiscal year (millions)
V-REV%Q	Percent change in revenue last quarter
V-REV%Y	Percent change in revenue year to date
V-EARN12	Earnings for last 12 months (millions)
V-GROWTH	5-year compounded growth rate
V-EARN%12	Percent change in earnings last 12 months
V-EARN%FY	Percent change in earnings year to date
V-EARN%Q	Percent change in earnings last quarter
V-EPSFY	Earnings per share last fiscal year
V-EPS12	Earnings per share last 12 months
V-DIVIDEND	Current dividend per share
V-DIVYLD	Dividend yield
V-DIVGRW	Dividend growth rate last 5 years
V-DIVPAYFY	Dividend payout last fiscal year
V-DIVPAY5Y	Dividend payout last 5 years
V-XDIV	Last ex-dividend date
V-CURR	Current ratio
V-INTCOV	Interest coverage
V-DEBTR	Long-term debt to equity ratio
V-REVR	Revenue to assets ratio
V-RETTA	Return on total assets
V-RETCE	Return on common equity
V-PMGIN	Profit margin last 12 months
V-MVAL	Market value of shares
V-SHARES	Shares outstanding
V-INSIDER	Net insider trading
V-SIR	Short interest ratio
V-FYEND	Ending month of fiscal year
V-CHNG1	Percent price change last week
V-CHNG4	Percent price change last 4 weeks
V-CHNG13	Percent price change last 13 weeks
V-CHNG52	Percent price change last 52 weeks
V-CHNGYTD	Percent price change year to date
V-CGSPYTD	Percent change vs. Standard and Poor's year to date
V-CGSP52	Percent change vs. Standard and Poor's last 52 weeks
V-CGSP13	Percent change vs. Standard and Poor's last 13 weeks
V-CGSP4	Percent change vs. Standard and Poor's last 4 weeks
V-CGSP1	Percent change vs. Standard and Poor's last week
V-HIGH52	52-week high

EXHIBIT 4–3 (*continued*)

V-LOW52	52-week low
V-HIGH5YR	5-year high
V-LOW5YR	5-year low
V-RPI	Relative price index
V-PRRPS	Price to revenue per share ratio
V-PREQ%	Price to common equity ratio
V-LOW5PER	5-year average low price earnings ratio
V-HIGH5PER	5-year average high price earnings ratio
V-CURRPER	Current price earnings ratio
V-BETAUP	Beta in up markets
V-BETADOWN	Beta in down markets
V-OBI	On balance index (relates share volume to up movement)
V-LQR	Liquidity ratio (relates $ volume to movement)
V-VOL%	Percentage of shares traded last week
V-VOL$	Dollar volume traded last week
V-VOLWK	Shares traded last week

DISCLOSURE II DATABASE:

V-CASH	Cash
V-SEC	Marketable securities
V-RECEIVE	Receivables
V-INVEN	Inventories
V-RAW	Raw materials
V-WIP	Work in progress
V-FINISH	Finished goods
V-NOTESR	Notes receivable
V-OCA	Other current assets
V-TCA	Total current assets
V-PPE	Property, plant, and equipment
V-DEP	Accumulated depreciation
V-NETPE	Net property and equipment
V-INVEST	Investment and advances to subsidiaries
V-NCA	Other noncurrent assets
V-DEFER	Deferred charges
V-INTANG	Intangibles
V-DEPOSITS	Deposits, other assets
V-ASSETS	Total assets
V-NOTEPAY	Notes payable
V-ACTPAY	Accounts payable
V-CURLT	Current long-term debt
V-CURCL	Current portion capital leases
V-ACCEXP	Accrued expenses
V-INCTAX	Income Taxes
V-OCL	Other current liabilities
V-TCL	Total current liabilities
V-MORT	Mortgages
V-DEF	Deferred charges
V-CONV	Convertible debt
V-LTD	Long-term debt

EXHIBIT 4–3 (*continued*)

V-NCL	Noncurrent capital leases
V-OLTL	Other long-term liabilities
V-LIAB	Total liabilities
V-MINOR	Minority interest
V-PREF	Preferred stock
V-COMMON	Common stock net
V-SURPLUS	Capital surplus
V-RETAIN	Retained earnings
V-TREAS	Treasury stock
V-OTHLIAB	Other liabilities
V-EQUITY	Shareholders' equity
V-WORTH	Total liabilities and net worth
V-SALES	Net sales
V-COST	Cost of goods
V-GROSS	Gross profit
V-R&D	R & D expenditures
V-SELL	Selling, general, and administrative expenses
V-GINC	Income before depreciation and amortization
V-DEPAM	Depreciation and amortization
V-NONOP	Nonoperating income
V-INTER	Interest expense
V-PTINC	Income before taxes
V-TAX	Provision for income taxes
V-MININT	Minority interest income
V-INVINC	Investment gains and losses
V-OTHINC	Other income
V-NETX	Net income before extraordinary items
V-EXTR	Extraordinary items and discontinued operations
V-NET	Net income
V-OUTSHR	Outstanding shares

CORPORATE EARNINGS ESTIMATOR:

V-MEANEST	Mean earnings per share estimate (current fiscal year)
V-HIGHEST	High earnings per share estimate (current fiscal year)
V-LOWEST	Low earnings per share estimate (current fiscal year)
V-NUMAN	Number of analysts (current fiscal year)
V-ESTPE	Estimated P/E ratio (current fiscal year)
V-WEEKEPS	Past earnings per share estimates - 1 week ago (current fiscal year)
V-13WKEPS	Past earnings per share estimates - 13 weeks ago (current fiscal year)
V-26WKEPS	Past earnings per share estimates - 26 weeks ago (current fiscal year)
V-NMEANEST	Mean earnings per share estimate (next fiscal year)
V-NHIGHEST	High earnings per share estimate (next fiscal year)
V-NLOWEST	Low earnings per share estimate (next fiscal year)

EXHIBIT 4–3 (*concluded*)

V-NNUMAN	Number of analysts (next fiscal year)
V-NESTPE	Estimated P/E ratio (next fiscal year)
V-NWEEKEPS	Past earnings per share estimate - 1 week ago (next fiscal year)
V-N13WKEPS	Past earnings per share estimates - 13 weeks ago (next fiscal year)
V-N26WKEPS	Past earnings per share estimates - 26 weeks ago (next fiscal year)

*Not available for over-the-counter stocks.
**Available for over-the-counter stocks only.
***Available for U.S. Treasury bonds only.

SOURCE: By permission of Dow Jones & Co., Inc.

---

plate for flaws that would cause errors during an on-line session with Dow Jones News/Retrieval. Upon completion of the edit, Dow Jones Spreadsheet Link automatically logs onto Dow Jones News/Retrieval, retrieves and stores the requested information, and logs off.

The information retrieved is not automatically stored in the spreadsheet template. It is stored in a file called DJ. To load the data into your template, you must reload the spreadsheet program, load the template you are using, and then load the data retrieved over it. The result is illustrated in Exhibit 4–4.

The value of using a spreadsheet link program, such as Dow Jones Spreadsheet Link, depends on the amount and type of information you require and how often you require it. However, if you find portfolio management software package report formats too rigid but you don't want to give up the capability to automatically retrieve data from an on-line service, a spreadsheet link program may be your solution.

Market Link

Market Link from Smith Micro Software, Inc., is a low cost alternative to Dow Jones Spreadsheet Link for investors who want to retrieve current price quotes only.

Market Link is, in essence, a communications program. It is designed to access Dow Jones News/Retrieval and The Source™

EXHIBIT 4–4 Spreadsheet Template after Data Is Retrieved from Dow Jones News/Retrieval

```
   : A :    B      : C  : D : E : F  :  G   :  H  :  I  :  J  :  K : L  :  M  :  N  :
 1:                                V-LAST
 2:
 3:                              J.P. INVESTOR
 4:
 5:                          PORTFOLIO STATUS REPORT
 6:
 7:                              24-Jan-86
 8:
 9:
10: --------------------------------------------------------------------------------
11:                                               UNREALIZED
12:                                               GAIN/LOSS
13:                       NUMBER COST        CURRENT        ------------------PERCENT          YIELD  YIELD ON
14: TICKER                  OF   PER  TOTAL PRICE PER CURRENT SHORT- LONG-  GAIN/ ANNUAL        ON    CURRENT
15: SYMBOL COMPANY NAME  DATE  SHARES SHARE  COST  SHARE  VALUE  TERM   TERM  LOSS  DIVIDEND     COST   VALUE
16: --------------------------------------------------------------------------------
17: V-GE   General Electric 14-Mar-77 100 25.13 2512.50  68.88  6887.50  0.00 4375.00 174%  2.20    8.76%  3.19%
18: V-IBM  Int'l Bus. Mach. 06-Jun-82 100 60.00 6000.00 150.88 15087.50  0.00 9087.50 151%  4.40    7.33%  2.92%
19: V-PEP  Pepsico          14-Mar-84 100 37.25 3725.00  69.88  6987.50  0.00 3262.50  88%  1.78    4.78%  2.55%
20: V-LOTS Lotus Dev. Corp. 26-Jul-85 200 28.75 5750.00  25.00  5000.00  0.00 -750.00 -13%  0.00    0.00%  0.00%
21: V-CMPQ Compaq Computer  09-Aug-85 200 10.38 2075.00  13.25  2650.00 575.00   0.00  28%  0.00    0.00%  0.00%
22: ...   ................. .......... ... ..... ....... ...... ....... ....... ....... ....  ....    .....  .....
23: ...   ................. .......... ... ..... ....... ...... ....... ....... ....... ....  ....    .....  .....
24: ...   ................. .......... ... ..... ....... ...... ....... ....... ....... ....  ....    .....  .....
25: ...   ................. .......... ... ..... ....... ...... ....... ....... ....... ....  ....    .....  .....
26: ...   ................. .......... ... ..... ....... ...... ....... ....... ....... ....  ....    .....  .....
27: --------------------------------------------------------------------------------
28:
29: TOTALS:                        20062.50        36612.50 575.00 15975.00  82%
30: ================================================================================
31:
32:
33:
```

to obtain current price quotes for up to 120 securities at a time, including stocks, bonds, options, mutual funds, and Treasury bills.

For each security, the open, high, low, and last price, and volume is automatically retrieved and stored on a disk in ASCII format. Spreadsheet users can subsequently convert the data to a file that can be used in a spreadsheet template. For example, with Lotus 1-2-3, users would use the /File Import command.

The program is straightforward and easy to use since virtually every function is controlled with one keystroke. The Main Menu contains six choices: system parameters, update symbol list, set/recall auto fetch, link to Dow Jones, link to The Source, and terminate run.

The first time you use Market Link, you must choose systems parameters to specify the type of equipment you are using, as well as telephone numbers and passwords used to access either Dow Jones News/Retrieval or The Source.

Update symbol list allows you to enter up to 120 security symbols which will be used for automatic retrieval of quotes.

When you select the set/recall auto fetch choice from the Main Menu, you have the ability to set up Market Link to immediately retrieve quotes for the securities included in your symbol list or to retrieve quotes at any of up to eight predefined times during the day or night. This unique feature enables you to analyze price and volume activity throughout the trading day. For example, if you want to monitor security prices on an hourly basis, you can instruct the program to retrieve quotes at 10 A.M., 11 A.M., 12 P.M., 1 P.M., 2 P.M., 3 P.M., and when the market closes at 4 P.M.

Market Link also includes a terminal mode that enables you to access all of the services available on Dow Jones News/Retrieval and The Source. The link to Dow Jones and link to The Source choices on the Main Menu are used for this purpose.

Market Link is limited to current quotes, but it performs without any difficulty if that is all you require.

CONCLUSION

Spreadsheet programs offer investors a great deal of flexibility in constructing the reports necessary to monitor their portfolios. Add to that the data retrieval capability of a spreadsheet link program and you may find them to be an attractive alternative to a portfolio management software package.

CHAPTER 5

On-Line Portfolio Management

An increasing number of investors are maintaining their portfolio records through an on-line service, such as CompuServe, The Source, and Schwab's Investor Information Service. The on-line portfolio management features are often sponsored by major discount brokerage firms, such as Charles Schwab & Co., Inc., and Quick & Reilly.

On-line portfolio management capabilities are very similar to those of portfolio management software. You enter information on the securities you own, and then, whenever you want a current status report of your holdings, you sign on to the on-line service, enter the name of your portfolio, and generate the appropriate report.

A significant difference between using portfolio management software and on-line portfolio management is that portfolio maintenance can be automated with the latter. For example, when you buy or sell a security through the on-line service, that information can be automatically recorded in your portfolio records, eliminating the need to enter such information manually.

SCHWAB'S INVESTOR INFORMATION SERVICE

As an example, let's examine Schwab's Investor Information Service, offered by the nation's largest discount broker, Charles Schwab & Co., Inc. To use Schwab's Investor Information Service, you must purchase The Equalizer® software from Schwab. It is available for both Apple II series personal computers and the IBM PC, XT, or AT (or true compatibles).

EXHIBIT 5–1   The Equalizer's Main Menu

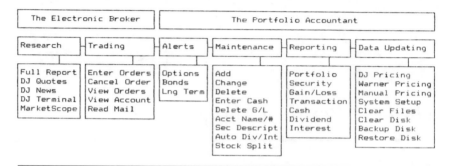

```
                Charles Schwab & Co., Inc. presents:

                         The Equalizer
```

The Electronic Broker		The Portfolio Accountant			
Research	Trading	Alerts	Maintenance	Reporting	Data Updating
Full Report	Enter Orders	Options	Add	Portfolio	DJ Pricing
DJ Quotes	Cancel Order	Bonds	Change	Security	Warner Pricing
DJ News	View Orders	Lng Term	Delete	Gain/Loss	Manual Pricing
DJ Terminal	View Account		Enter Cash	Transaction	System Setup
MarketScope	Read Mail		Delete G/L	Cash	Clear Files
			Acct Name/#	Dividend	Clear Disk
			Sec Descript	Interest	Backup Disk
			Auto Div/Int		Restore Disk
			Stock Split		

Using The Equalizer,® you can access Schwab's Investor Information Service to do research, initiate trades, and manage your investments in the comfort of your home. As shown in Exhibit 5–1, The Equalizer is divided into two main sections, one for strategic decision making and the other for efficient record keeping.

The decision making section consists of research and trading, while the record keeping section is comprised of alerts, maintenance, reporting and data updating. The research capability is discussed in Chapter 8, while the others will be discussed here.

On-Line Trading

For the most part, there is very little difference between one on-line trading system and another, and, for that matter, there is no reason why there should be. Schwab's On-Line Trading System enables you to enter or cancel orders, view your open orders and account information, receive notification of all trades executed by Schwab, and update your portfolio when trades are executed.

The mechanics of placing an order involve entering a one-letter portfolio code for the portfolio you want to trade in, indicating whether you want to buy or sell, and identifying the type of security. You also need to identify the security symbol, the number of shares or contracts (if you are trading options), the highest price you are willing to pay if you are buying or the lowest price you are willing to receive if you are selling, and whether the

EXHIBIT 5–2   The Equalizer's Order Entry Screen

The Equalizer: Enter Orders

Portfolio:	Name:					Acct No:		
% Equity in Margin Account: Cash Account Balance: Money Market Funds Available:						Margin Account Equity: Margin Cash Available:		
Port	B/S	Symbol	Type	O/ C	Security Description	Qty	Price	Day/ GTC

F1Enter Orders F2Cancel Orders F3View Orders F4View Account F5Read Mail

order is good for that day only or until you cancel it. Exhibit 5–2 shows The Equalizer's order entry screen.

After you enter the required order information, you must enter your trading password. The trading password is a security measure to safeguard against unauthorized access to your Schwab account.

Next, The Equalizer automatically signs on to the Schwab On-Line Trading System through a local telephone access number. It then displays information about your trade, including a restatement of your order, your current position in the security according to Schwab's records, a real-time quote for the security, the estimated commission for the trade, and the estimated cost of a buy or proceeds of a sell. After reviewing the information, you have one last chance to change your mind. You can either change the order or delete it entirely.

If you decide to place the order, you will get a message confirming that Schwab has received it. And, as soon as the trade is executed, notification will be sent to your electronic mailbox. If your account is set up for on-line trading, you will receive notification of all trade executions in your electronic mailbox, regardless of whether your order was placed through your computer or verbally over the telephone.

You pay no charges for being connected to the Schwab On-Line Trading System. This encourages use of the system. After all, if you have made a deliberate choice to save commission costs by using a discount broker, why would you be willing to pay on-line charges for placing orders when you could just as easily place the order over the telephone?

You may be asking yourself why you bother with on-line trading at all. Isn't it a nuisance to have to turn on the computer, wait until the program is loaded, and type in all of the information just to place an order? If you have ever missed out on an investment opportunity because you couldn't reach your broker by phone, you will appreciate how convenient placing orders on-line can be. In the current highly volatile stock market a few minutes can make a big difference.

The other advantages of on-line trading include the ability to access your account information at your convenience, quickly check for order executions, and automatically update your portfolio.

Alerts

You can obtain three different types of alerts useful for managing your investments. The first lists all options in your portfolio that will expire within any range of dates you specify. The second alert lists all bonds that will mature within your specified range of dates. The final alert identifies all securities in your portfolio that have gone, or will go, long-term within a given range of dates.

Portfolio Maintenance

The Equalizer's portfolio maintenance feature enables you to add, change, or delete securities from your portfolios, record dividends and interest received, enter or withdraw cash from individual portfolios, and perform a variety of other functions that help manage your portfolios. The information required to add securities is illustrated in Exhibit 5–3. Similar information is required to change or delete securities from your portfolio.

The Equalizer allows you to set up and maintain up to 26 separate portfolios. Each portfolio can contain real or imaginary holdings so you can track securities you are interested in but do not currently own separately from your actual holdings.

Reports

Reports are key to portfolio management, whether you are monitoring your portfolio manually or using software or an on-line

EXHIBIT 5–3   The Equalizer's Add Transactions Input Screen

```
                    The Equalizer:   Add Transactions

Portfolio: B      Name: SCHWAB ONE              Acct No: 79396427

          B                                   Price per
  Date    SS Symbol        Name     Quantity  Share     Comm.    Amount

02/01/85  B  BAC    BANKAMERICA CORP.  1000.000  18.75000  180.00   18930.00
```

```
                    Enter to accept transaction
    F1Add F2Change F3Delete F4Cash F5Del G/L F6Acct Info F7Sec Info F8Div F9Split
```

system. The reporting module of The Equalizer allows you to generate seven reports. These reports include a Holdings by Portfolio Report, Holdings by Security Report, Realized Gain/Loss Report, Security and Cash Transaction Report, Cash Transaction Report, Dividend Tax Report, and Interest Tax Report. Each report can be generated for a specific portfolio or for all of your portfolios in aggregate. A sample of each report is provided in Exhibits 5–4 to 5–10.

Data Updating

The data updating module enables you to update the prices of the securities in your portfolios, define your communications parameters, and perform disk maintenance. When pricing out one or more of your portfolios, current prices can be automatically retrieved from Dow Jones News/Retrieval or Warner Computer Systems. If you prefer, you can enter prices manually.

CONCLUSION

Schwab's Investor Information Service is typical of on-line portfolio management systems that allow you to place buy and sell orders for securities and monitor your portfolio on-line. For the individual investor, on-line portfolio management offers an attractive alternative to using portfolio management software.

EXHIBIT 5—4 Sample Holdings by Portfolio Report

```
                        Holdings by Portfolio Report

                                02/01/85

Portfolio: A   Name: SCHWAB ONE               Y-T-D Comm:            958.22
               Acct No: 79396427              Cash Balance:  1,701,728.03
===============================================================================
Security Name                   Buy Price Curr Price      Gain/Loss
Date                   Quantity Total Cost Curr Value   Long        Short    % G/L
-------------------- --------- ---------- ---------- ---------- ---------- ------

APPLE COMPUTER                    18.875     29.000
01/23/85                 1000   18900.00   29000.00  07/24/85   10100.00   53.44


-------------------- --------- ---------- ---------- ---------- ---------- ------

BANKAMERICA CORP.                 18.000     18.875
02/01/85                   70    1284.50    1321.25  08/02/85      36.75    2.86

BANKAMERICA CORP.                 17.750     18.875
02/01/85                 3000   53278.00   56625.00  08/02/85    3347.00    6.28

BANKAMERICA CORP.                 17.756     18.875
Total Long:              3070   54562.50   57946.25     ---      3383.75    6.20

-------------------- --------- ---------- ---------- ---------- ---------- ------

IBM                              108.875    133.625
11/18/84                10000 1088827.25 1336250.00  05/19/85  247422.75   22.72

IBM                              122.500    133.625
01/09/85                  100   12365.25   13362.50  07/10/85     997.25    8.06

IBM                              109.010    133.625
Total Long:             10100 1101192.50 1349612.50     ---    248420.00   22.56

-------------------- --------- ---------- ---------- ---------- ---------- ------

ROCKWELL INTL INC                 45.000     34.375
04/15/83                 7700  346500.00  264687.50 -81812.50      ---    -23.61

-------------------- --------- ---------- ---------- ---------- ---------- ------

TELEDYNE INC                     204.250    256.500
07/16/84                 1000  204358.00  256500.00  52142.00      ---     25.52

-------------------- --------- ---------- ---------- ---------- ---------- ------

Portfolio A Buys               1725513.00 1957746.25 -29670.50  261903.75  13.46

Portfolio Value:  256,018.22
```

EXHIBIT 5–5 Sample Holdings by Security Report

```
                      Holdings by Security Report

                             02/01/85

                                                            Page 1
===================================================================================
Portfolio Name                Buy Price  Curr Price      Gain/Loss
Date                 Quantity Total Cost Curr Value     Long       Short     % G/L
-------------------  -------- ---------- ----------  ---------- ----------  ------
* * * * * * * * * * * * * * *  APPLE COMPUTER  * * * * * * * * * * * * * * * * *

SCHWAB ONE                      18.875     29.000
01/23/85                1000   18900.00   29000.00   07/24/85   10100.00   53.44

* * * * * * * * * * * * * * *  BANKAMERICA CORP. * * * * * * * * * * * * * * * * *

INCOME                          18.750     18.875
02/01/85                1000   18865.25   18875.00   08/02/85       9.75     .05

SCHWAB ONE                      18.000     18.875
02/01/85                  70    1284.50    1321.25   08/02/85      36.75    2.86

SCHWAB ONE                      17.750     18.875
02/01/85                3000   53278.00   56625.00   08/02/85    3347.00    6.28

BANKAMERICA CORP.               18.000     18.875
Total Long:             4070   73427.75   76821.25      ---      3393.50    4.62

* * * * * * * * * * * * * * *  * *  IBM  * * * * * * * * * * * * * * * * * * * * *

SCHWAB ONE                     108.875    133.625
11/18/84               10000 1088827.25 1336250.00   05/19/85  247422.75   22.72

SCHWAB ONE                     122.500    133.625
01/09/85                 100   12365.25   13362.50   07/10/85     997.25    8.06

IBM                            109.010    133.625
Total Long:            10100 1101192.50 1349612.50      ---    248420.00   22.56

* * * * * * * * * * * * * * *  ROCKWELL INTL INC  * * * * * * * * * * * * * * *

SCHWAB ONE                      45.000     34.375
04/15/83                7700  346500.00  264687.50  -81812.50      ---    -23.61

* * * * * * * * * * * * * * * * TELEDYNE INC * * * * * * * * * * * * * * * * * * *

SCHWAB ONE                     204.250    256.500
07/16/84                1000  204358.00  256500.00   52142.00      ---     25.52

* * * * * * * * * * * * * * * * * * * * * * *  * * * * * * * * * * * * * * * * * *
```

EXHIBIT 5-6 Sample Realized Gain/Loss Report

```
                        Realized Gain/Loss Report

                        From 01/01/84 to 02/01/85

Portfolio: A  Name: SCHWAB ONE              Y-T-D Comm:          958.22
              Acct No: 79396427             Cash Balance:  1,701,728.03
================================================================================
     S       ********Buy********  ********Sell******  Total   Gain/Loss
Quant I Symbl  Date    Amount     Date     Amount     Comm   Long    Short
------ ------ -------- ---------- -------- ---------- ------- ------- -------
  100 IBM    01/09/85  12550.00  01/30/85  13250.00  245.75   ---    754.25
   30 BAC    02/01/85    532.50  02/01/85    562.50   21.75   ---      8.25
   20 BAC    02/01/85    355.00  02/01/85    375.00   14.50   ---      5.50


  150                  13137.50            14187.50  282.00   ---    768.00
```

EXHIBIT 5-7 Sample Security and Cash Transaction Report

```
                  Security and Cash Transaction Report

                        From 01/01/84 to 02/01/85

Portfolio: A  Name: SCHWAB ONE              Y-T-D Comm:          958.22
              Acct No: 79396427             Cash Balance:  1,701,728.03
================================================================================
Type    Date            Description         Commission   Amount    FSM12
------  --------  ------------------------  ----------  ----------  -----
Buy     01/21/85    200 TDY   @ 253.250        ---      -50,650.00
Buy     01/23/85   1000 BAC   @  17.750        ---      -17,750.00
Buy     01/23/85    150 TDY   @ 253.000        ---      -37,950.00
Buy     01/23/85   3500 XON   @  48.000        ---     -168,000.00
Buy     01/23/85   2100 CBU   @  12.750      30.00      -26,805.00
Sell    01/23/85   1000 CBU   @  13.875      25.00       13,850.00
Buy     01/23/85  10000 MITIZ @   8.000      30.00      -80,030.00
Buy     01/23/85   1200 IBM   @ 121.000      45.00     -145,245.00
Sell    01/23/85    800 IBM   @ 129.250      30.00      103,370.00
Div     07/29/84  DIV CHECK FM IBM STK         ---         225.34  F
Rcr     01/23/85    800 IBM   @ 121.000 01/23/85  30.00  -96,830.00
Sell    01/23/85    400 IBM   @ 129.000        ---       51,600.00
Sell    01/23/85    600 IBM   @ 129.000        ---       77,400.00
Short   01/23/85   1000 TDY   @ 266.000        ---      266,000.00
Short   01/23/85     25 ASAQJ @   7.000        ---       17,500.00
Short   01/15/85    100 AAPL  @  30.000      250.00       2,750.00
Delete  02/01/84    100 AAPL  @  30.000 01/15/85 250.00  -2,750.00
Delete  02/01/85   1000 BAC   @  17.750 02/01/85  ---    17,750.00
Delete  02/01/85    200 BAC   @ 253.250 02/01/85  ---    50,650.00
Buy     02/01/85    100 BAC   @  17.750      35.00       -1,810.00
Buy     02/01/85    100 BAC   @  17.750      35.00       -1,810.00
Sell    02/01/85     30 BAC   @  18.750      11.25          551.25
Sell    02/01/85     20 BAC   @  18.750       7.50          367.50
Buy     01/23/85    250 AAPL  @  27.500     137.50       -7,012.50
Buy     01/09/85    100 IBM   @ 122.500     115.25      -12,365.25
Change  02/01/85    250 AAPL  @  27.500 01/23/85 71.50   -6,946.50
Cash    01/03/85  Check #112 Deposit           ---       25,000.00  FSM12
Div     01/31/85  BAC Dividend                 ---        1,578.75
```

EXHIBIT 5-8   Sample Cash Transaction Report

```
                          Cash Transaction Report

                          From 01/01/84 to 02/01/85

Portfolio: A  Name: SCHWAB ONE              Y-T-D Comm:          958.22
              Acct No: 79396427             Cash Balance:  1,701,728.03
=======================================================================
                                                     Exempt
Type   Date      Description             Amount       Amount     FSM12
----   --------  -----------------------  -----------  ----------- -----
Div   07/29/84  DIV CHECK FM IBM STK         225.34       225.34 F
Cash  01/03/85  Check #112 Deposite       25,000.00    25,000.00 FSM12
Div   01/31/85  BAC Dividen                1,578.75       ---
Div   01/15/85  Div from Municipal bond    2,350.32     2,350.32 SM
Cash  01/03/85  Transfered from BAC       25,000.00       ---
Int   01/17/85  Interest, Municipal bond   2,365.78     2,365.78 SM

Portfolio A  Totals:                      56,520.19    25,225.34 Federal
                                                       29,716.10 State
                                                       29,716.10 Municpl
                                                       25,000.00 Other1
                                                       25,000.00 Other2
```

EXHIBIT 5-9   Sample Dividend Tax Report

```
                          Dividend Tax Report

                          From 01/01/84 to 02/01/85

Portfolio: A  Name: SCHWAB ONE              Y-T-D Comm:          958.22
              Acct No: 79396427             Cash Balance:  1,701,728.03
=======================================================================
                                                     Exempt
Type   Date      Description             Amount       Amount     FSM12
----   --------  -----------------------  -----------  ----------- -----
Div   07/29/84  DIV CHECK FM IBM STK         225.34       225.34 F
Div   01/31/85  BAC Dividen                1,578.75       ---
Div   01/15/85  Div from Municipal bond    2,350.32     2,350.32 SM

Portfolio A  Totals:                       4,154.41       225.34 Federal
                                                        2,350.32 State
                                                        2,350.32 Municpl
                                                           ---    Other1
                                                           ---    Other2
```

EXHIBIT 5–10 Sample Interest Tax Report

```
                       Interest Tax Report

                   From 01/01/84 to 02/01/85

Portfolio: A  Name: SCHWAB ONE                Y-T-D Comm:          958.22
              Acct No: 79396427               Cash Balance:  1,701,728.03
========================================================================
                                                        Exempt
Type   Date           Description          Amount        Amount   FSM12
----   --------   -------------------------   ------------   ------------   -----
Int   01/17/85   Interest,Municipal bond     2,365.78     2,365.78  SM

Portfolio A  Totals:                         2,365.78          ---  Federal
                                                          2,365.78  State
                                                          2,365.78  Municpl
                                                               ---  Other1
                                                               ---  Other2
```

PART 3

Fundamental Analysis

CHAPTER 6

Stock Screening

It seems like everytime you pick up a newspaper, you read about one big company taking over another with the stockholders of the latter reaping a huge profit overnight. Recently, General Electric offered RCA stockholders $66.50 per share, and, in the week the takeover was announced, RCA's stock shot up from $47.25 to $59.63 per share—a staggering 26 percent gain.

Why does this happen over and over again? The basic reason is that the acquiring company believes that the stock price of the company they want to buy does not represent its real worth in cash, assets, and earnings. They feel that the company is undervalued and can be picked up at a bargain. In the case of RCA, many Wall Street analysts felt the real value of RCA was in excess of $75 per share; therefore, at $66.50 per share RCA represented a bargain to General Electric.

In essence, this is what fundamental analysis is all about. Fundamentalists, as those performing fundamental analysis are called, are simply looking for a bargain—stock that is selling at a price that doesn't represent the real worth of the company.

Does that mean that everytime you buy a company's stock that seems to be undervalued another company is going to come along and snap it up at a higher price? No, but it does mean that if the numbers being used to evaluate the company are accurate and they indicate that the company's stock is undervalued, the odds are that over time the stock's price will move higher and you will be able to sell the stock for more than you paid for it.

How do you find undervalued stocks? One way is to evaluate a group of stocks and identify those that meet a predefined set of criteria that indicate undervaluation.

For example, you might look for stocks listed on the New York Stock Exchange with a stock price less than book value per share. Alternatively, you might want to locate stocks with a price/earnings ratio of less than 10, dividend yield greater than 10 percent, and an increase in sales from the prior year of greater than 10 percent. There is no magic formula to the criteria you select. A wide range of criteria can be used to find undervalued stocks.

How long will it take to identify the stocks meeting your conditions? Regardless of the criteria you use, if you attempt to identify particular stocks from the tens of thousands of stocks traded by looking through newspapers, annual reports, investment services, and other sources of printed information, it will take you hours, if not days.

The time required to perform research has long been recognized as a major factor limiting the amount of fundamental analysis both individual and professional investors could perform. That time constraint has been eliminated with the advent of the personal computer and fundamental analysis software packages. Now, both individual and professional investors have access to huge databases containing key information on thousands of stocks. This makes serious fundamental analysis easy. And, given the speed at which the personal computer can manipulate data, identifying particular stocks meeting your criteria now takes only minutes, not days.

SELECTING FUNDAMENTAL ANALYSIS SOFTWARE

A number of considerations are important in selecting a fundamental analysis software package that meets your needs. A good way to compare alternative packages is to complete the questionnaire provided in Exhibit 6–1 for each package. The questionnaire ensures that you have looked at all the important considerations about fundamental analysis software. Exhibit 6–2 shows a completed fundamental analysis software questionnaire for Stockpak II, a leading stock screening software package.

Remember, it will take time to evaluate the various software packages to make sure you buy software that meets your specific needs. In the long run, the benefit you receive from using the right package will make this process worth the effort.

Understandably, there are a limited number of fundamental analysis software packages on the market. Most of these packages

---

EXHIBIT 6–1   Fundamental Analysis Software Questionnaire—IBM PC
Systems

GENERAL INFORMATION

Product name: _____   Version #: _____
Vendor name: _____
Address: _____
_____
_____
Telephone: _____
List price: _____
Demonstration diskette available?   _____ Yes   _____ No
    If yes, what is the price of the demonstration diskette? _____
Money-back guarantee available?   _____ Yes   _____ No
    If yes, how many days? _____

HARDWARE REQUIREMENTS

Operating system: _____ DOS 1.1 or later   _____Other (Specify) _____
               _____ DOS 2.0 or later
Minimum memory required: ____ 64K ____ 128K ____ 192K ____ 256K
Number of disk drives required: _____ 1 single-sided
                                _____ 2 single-sided
                                _____ 1 double-sided
                                _____ 2 double-sided
                        Other _____
Color graphics required?   _____ Yes   _____ No
Modem required?   _____ Yes   _____ No
Modem recommended?   _____ Yes   _____ No
Printer required?   _____ Yes   _____ No
Printer recommended?   _____ Yes   _____ No
Other hardware requirements (specify): _____
_____
_____
_____

PRODUCT SUPPORT
Who provides support for the product? _____
Is there a telephone number available for support?   _____ Yes   _____ No
    If yes, is it toll-free?   _____ Yes   _____ No
    Days of the week support is available: _____
    Hours of the day support is available: _____
Is the software copy protected?   _____ Yes   _____ No
    If yes, can you copy program to a hard disk?   _____ Yes   _____ No
    Cost of backup copy? _____
Defective disk replacement policy: _____
_____
_____
_____

Update policy: _____
_____
_____
_____

EXHIBIT 6–1 (*continued*)

DOCUMENTATION

Number of pages in user's manual? _____

User's manual includes:	Yes	No
Tutorial	___	___
Index	___	___
Glossary	___	___
Explanation of error messages	___	___
Sample applications	___	___
Samples of screen displays	___	___
Samples of printed output	___	___

Does the package include a tutorial on disk? ___ Yes ___ No
Does the package include a reference card? ___ Yes ___ No
Does the disk contain sample applications? ___ Yes ___ No
    If yes, how many and what type? _____
Does the package include a demonstration disk? ___ Yes ___ No

EASE OF USE

Estimated time to learn basic functions:
___ Less than 1 day ___ 1 to 6 days ___ 1 to 2 weeks
___ Over 2 weeks
Commands are abbreviated for quick entry? ___ Yes ___ No
Error messages are provided on screen? ___ Yes ___ No
Programs are menu driven? ___ Yes ___ No
Help screens are available? ___ At all times
                                ___ At various points in the program
                                ___ Nonexistent
How experienced with the IBM PC should a person be to use this package?
___ Very ___ Somewhat ___ Little ___ No experience

SCREENING CAPABILITIES

Is this a stock screening package? ___ Yes ___ No
    (If no, go to OTHER CAPABILITIES below).
Does the software access a disk containing fundamental data on companies?
    ___ Yes ___ No
    If yes, answer the following five questions:
    How many disks? _____
    How many companies are included on one disk? _____
    How many industry groups are included on one disk? _____
    From which stock exchanges are companies listed? (Check all that apply)
    ___ New York Stock Exchange
    ___ American Stock Exchange
    ___ NASDAQ
    ___ Other (Specify) _____
    What is the frequency of updates? _____
Does the software access an on-line database for items to be screened?
    ___ Yes ___ No
    If yes, which on-line database is accessed? (Check all that apply)
    ___ Dow Jones News/Retrieval
    ___ Other (Specify) _____
    How many items are available for screening? _____

EXHIBIT 6–1 (*continued*)

Which of the following types of information are included as items available for screening? (Check all that apply)
_____ Market price
_____ Earnings
_____ Sales
_____ Beta
_____ Dividends
_____ Assets
_____ Liabilities
_____ Financial ratios
_____ Proprietary items (Specify) _____

_____

_____ Other (Specify) _____
_____ Other (Specify) _____
Can the user combine items available for screening using formulae?
_____ Yes _____ No
Can the user enter items to be used for screening in addition to those
already in the database? _____ Yes _____ No
If yes, how many? _____
What is the maximum number of items that can be used in screening? _____
Can the user specify ranges and limits for each screening criteria?
_____ Yes _____ No
Can screening results be saved on disk? _____ Yes _____ No
Can screening and sorting criteria be saved on disk? _____ Yes _____ No
Can reports be generated on the screen? _____ Yes _____ No
Can reports be printed? _____ Yes _____ No
Are there fixed report formats? _____ Yes _____ No
If yes, how many? _____
Can users define report formats? _____ Yes _____ No
List the types of reports that can be generated:

_____

_____

_____

_____

_____

_____

OTHER CAPABILITIES
Is the software based on a particular fundamentalist approach to the stock
market? _____ Yes _____ No
If yes, briefly describe the approach:

_____

_____

_____

Is the user prompted for data to be entered? _____ Yes _____ No

EXHIBIT 6–1 *(concluded)*

What items of data are entered by the user?

_____

_____

_____

_____

_____

Are the necessary data items readily available to users?
_____ Yes _____ No
Can the user access an on-line database for required data items?
_____ Yes _____ No
If yes, which on-line database is accessed? (Check all that apply)
_____ Dow Jones News/Retrieval
_____ Warner Computer Systems
_____ Other (Specify) _____
After data is entered, can it be easily checked and changed?
_____ Yes _____ No
List the types of reports that can be generated:

_____

_____

_____

_____

_____

_____

_____

EXHIBIT 6–2 Completed Fundamental Analysis Software Questionnaire for
Stockpak II—IBM PC Version

GENERAL INFORMATION

Product name: Stockpak II _____ Version #: N/A* _____
Vendor name: Standard & Poor's Corporation
Address: 25 Broadway _____
New York, NY 10004 _____

Telephone: (212) 208–8581 _____
List price: Depends upon subscription:
(1) All NYSE stocks $275/year
(2) All AMEX stocks $275/year
(3) All OTC stocks $520/year
(4) Composite of NYSE, AMEX,
and OTC stocks $275/year
Demonstration diskette available? _X_ Yes _____ No
If yes, what is the price of the demonstration diskette? $10.00 _____

EXHIBIT 6–2 (*continued*)

Money-back guarantee available? _____ Yes _X_ No
    If yes, how many days?   N/A_____

HARDWARE REQUIREMENTS

Operating system: _____ DOS 1.1 or later _X_ Other (Specify) FORTH_____
    _____ DOS 2.0 or later
Minimum memory required: _____ 64K _X_ 128K _____ 192K _____ 256K
Number of disk drives required: _X_ 1 single-sided
                               _____ 2 single-sided
                               _____ 1 double-sided
                               _____ 2 double-sided
                               Other _____
Color graphics required? _____ Yes _X_ No
Modem required? _____ Yes _X_ No
Modem recommended? _____ Yes _X_ No
Printer required? _____ Yes _X_ No
Printer recommended? _X_ Yes _____ No
Other hardware requirements (specify): None_____
_____
_____
_____

PRODUCT SUPPORT

Who provides support for the product? Standard & Poor's Corporation_____
Is there a telephone number available for support? _____ Yes _X_ No
    If yes, is it toll-free? _____ Yes _X_ No   The manual indicates
        that for further assistance write S&P - Micro Services Division
    Days of the week support is available: N/A_____
    Hours of the day support is available: N/A_____
Is the software copy protected? _____ Yes _X_ No
    If yes, can you copy program to a hard disk? N/A Yes _____ No
    Cost of backup copy? N/A_____
Defective disk replacement policy: Standard & Poor's will replace defective
    disks for a period of 90 days from date of purchase free of charge.
    After 90 days, a replacement fee is charged._____

Update policy: No update policy is indicated._____
_____
_____

DOCUMENTATION

Number of pages in user's manual? _____59_____
User's manual includes: Yes   No
    Tutorial   _____   _X_
    Index   _____   _X_
    Glossary   _____   _X_
    Explanation of error messages   _____   _X_

EXHIBIT 6–2 (*continued*)

Sample applications   _____   _X_
Samples of screen displays   _X_   _____
Samples of printed output   _X_   _____
Does the package include a tutorial on disk?   _____ Yes   _X_ No
Does the package include a reference card?   _____ Yes   _X_ No
Does the disk contain sample applications?   _____ Yes   _X_ No
    If yes, how many and what type? _N/A_____
Does the package include a demonstration disk?   _____ Yes   _X_ No

EASE OF USE
Estimated time to learn basic functions:
   _X_ Less than 1 day   _____ 1 to 6 days   _____ 1 to 2 weeks
   _____ Over 2 weeks
Commands are abbreviated for quick entry?   _X_ Yes   _____ No
Error messages are provided on screen?   _X_ Yes   _____ No
Programs are menu driven?   _X_ Yes   _____ No
Help screens are available?   _____ At all times
                                _____ At various points in the program
                                _X_ Nonexistent
How experienced with the IBM PC should a person be to use this package?
   _____ Very   _____ Somewhat   _X_ Little   _____ No experience

SCREENING CAPABILITIES
Is this a stock screening package?   _X_ Yes   _____ No
    (If no, go to OTHER CAPABILITIES below).
Does the software access a disk containing fundamental data on companies?
   _X_ Yes   _____ No
    If yes, answer the following four questions:

(1) NYSE subscription:
    How many disks? _____1_____
    How many companies are included on one disk? _1,500_____
    How many industry groups are included on one disk? _Information is_____
    organized by company not industry._____
    From which stock exchanges are companies listed? (Check all that apply)
    _X_ New York Stock Exchange
    _____ American Stock Exchange
    _____ NASDAQ
    _____ Other (Specify) _____

(2) AMEX subscription:
    How many disks? _____1_____
    How many companies are included on one disk? _800_____
    How many industry groups are included on one disk? _Information is_____
    organized by company not industry._____

EXHIBIT 6–2 (*continued*)

From which stock exchanges are companies listed? (Check all that apply)
_____ New York Stock Exchange
__X__ American Stock Exchange
_____ NASDAQ
_____ Other (Specify) _____

(3) NASDAQ subscription:

How many disks? ___2___
How many companies are included on one disk? ____Total of 2,200____
How many industry groups are included on one disk? _Information is_____
organized by company not industry._____
From which stock exchanges are companies listed? (Check all that apply)
_____ New York Stock Exchange
_____ American Stock Exchange
__X__ NASDAQ
_____ Other (Specify) _____

(4) Composite subscription:

How many disks? ____1____
How many companies are included on one disk? _1,500_____
How many industry groups are included on one disk? _Information is_____
organized by company not industry._____
From which stock exchanges are companies listed? (Check all that apply)
__X__ New York Stock Exchange
__X__ American Stock Exchange
__X__ NASDAQ
_____ Other (Specify) _____
What is the frequency of updates? _Monthly_____
Does the software access an on-line database for items to be screened?
_____ Yes __X__ No
If yes, which on-line database is accessed? (Check all that apply)
N/A _____ Dow Jones News/Retrieval
_____ Other (Specify) _____
How many items are available for screening? _108 (83 data_ items plus 25
the user can define)
Which of the following types of information are included as items available for
screening? (Check all that apply)
__X__ Market price
__X__ Earnings
__X__ Sales
__X__ Beta
__X__ Dividends
__X__ Assets
__X__ Liabilities
__X__ Financial ratios

EXHIBIT 6–2 *(continued)*

__X__ Proprietary items (Specify) <u>Standard & Poor's</u>
<u>Stock Ranking</u>

_____ Other (Specify) _____
_____ Other (Specify) _____
Can the user combine items available for screening using formulae?
__X__ Yes _____ No
Can the user enter items to be used for screening in addition to those
already in the database? __X__ Yes _____ No
If yes, how many? __25__
What is the maximum number of items that can be used
in screening? __7__
Can the user specify ranges and limits for each screening criteria?
__X__ Yes _____ No
Can screening results be saved on disk? __X__ Yes _____ No
Can screening and sorting criteria be saved on disk? __X__ Yes _____ No
Can reports be generated on the screen? __X__ Yes _____ No
Can reports be printed? __X__ Yes _____ No
Are there fixed report formats? __X__ Yes _____ No
If yes, how many? __10__
Can users define report formats? __X__ Yes _____ No
List the types of reports that can be generated:
   (1) Report containing all of the data items for an individual company.
   (2) Graphic display of earnings and sales data for an individual company.
   (3) Report comparing user specified data items for more than
      one company.
   (4) Results of screening process.
   (5) Up to 10 predefined report formats or other user defined report formats
      can be used to compare companies meeting screening criteria.

OTHER CAPABILITIES
Is the software based on a particular fundamentalist approach to the stock
market? __N/A__ Yes _____ No
If yes, briefly describe the approach:
N/A

Is the user prompted for data to be entered? N/A _____ Yes _____ No
What items of data are entered by the user? N/A

EXHIBIT 6–2 (*concluded*)

_____

_____

Are the necessary data items readily available to users? N/A
_____ Yes _____ No
Can the user access an on-line database for required data items? N/A
_____ Yes _____ No
   If yes, which on-line database is accessed? (Check all that apply)
   _____ Dow Jones News/Retrieval   N/A
   _____ Warner Computer Systems
   _____ Other (Specify) _____
After data is entered, can it be easily checked and changed?   N/A
_____ Yes _____ No
List the types of reports that can be generated: N/A

_____

_____

_____

_____

_____

_____

_____

*N/A = not applicable.

require access to an extensive database of financial information, either on a disk or on-line. Building and maintaining such a database is no easy task and most vendors cannot justify its cost unless the database can also be used for other purposes.

For that reason, most of the fundamental analysis software packages are offered by companies that not only provide the financial information on disk or in an on-line database, but also provide the information in one or more printed forms. These vendors include such well respected names as Standard & Poor's Corporation, and Value Line, Inc.

STOCK SCREENING SOFTWARE

The majority of fundamental analysis software packages are called stock screening packages. Stock screening packages do exactly what the name implies. They screen through a large group of stocks and identify only those meeting conditions that you specify.

For example, you might want to identify all stocks listed on the New York Stock Exchange having a market price per share less than book value per share and a dividend yield greater than 10 percent. Using a stock screening package, you can narrow down your choice of stocks from the thousands available to a handful; as of December 1985, there were only nine stocks meeting the criteria described.

Financial information on the stocks can be included on a disk or accessed from an on-line database, such as CompuServe. In the case where the data is on a disk, you would receive a new data disk containing up-to-date information on a periodic basis, normally monthly. Where you access an on-line database, the data is normally updated on a continuous basis and is more current.

You will incur an ongoing charge with the stock screening packages. If you use a package that accesses data on a disk, you will have to pay an annual subscription fee, much like you do for a magazine or a newsletter. On the other hand, if you access an on-line database, you will have to pay only for the time you are connected to the service each time you retrieve data.

The amount and type of data available for screening varies with the software package you are using and the source of the data. For example, with Standard & Poor's Stockpak II, you have a choice of four different databases on disks that you can subscribe to. One database contains about 1,500 stocks listed on the New

York Stock Exchange, while another is comprised of the same number of stocks listed on the American Stock Exchange. A third includes two disks and contains a total of 2,200 over-the-counter stocks. Finally, a composite database offers information on 1,500 leading companies whose stocks are listed on the New York Stock Exchange and American Stock Exchange, or sold in the over-the-counter market.

Each Stockpak II database disk contains 83 predefined data items on each company including Standard & Poor's proprietary ranking for each company and earnings per share estimates.

With Value Line's Value/Screen Plus™, only one database disk is available. That disk contains information on more than 1,600 stocks, which account for more than 95 percent of the stock trading activity on all U.S. stock exchanges. The data disk contains 37 predefined data items for each stock including historical growth rates, measures of current performance and volatility, and key projections. In addition, Value Line's proprietary rankings for timeliness and safety are included.

Key Features

When selecting a stock screening software package, you should keep in mind the type of data you want to use for screening stocks and the form you want the data in, either on a disk or on-line.

In evaluating each stock screening software package, you need to answer a wide range of questions. For each software package, determine the number of companies and industries that can be screened, on which stock exchanges the companies are listed, and the frequency at which data is updated. In addition, identify exactly what types of information can be screened, including market price, earnings, sales, beta, dividends, assets, liabilities, financial ratios, and proprietary items.

You should also determine if you can combine items available for screening. It can be advantageous to be able to combine two or more of the items to create a new financial ratio or constant that can also be used for screening purposes. This, in essence, dramatically expands the number of items that can be screened.

To ensure that you have the capability to create very precise screens, the maximum number of items that can be used for screening is also a key factor. Although there is no magic number of screening criteria that should be available, a minimum of five is recommended.

In addition, for each screening criteria, you should be able to specify ranges and limits. For example, if you are screening for stocks with low price/earnings ratios, you should be able to enter a range of greater than zero but less than six.

A final valuable capability is being able to print reports in user-defined formats in addition to predefined formats. This gives you the flexibility to include only items that are important to you.

Let's look at three different stock screenings, Standard & Poor's Stockpak II, Value Line's Value/Screen Plus, and CompuServe's security screening feature.

Screening Stocks with Stockpak II

Standard & Poor's Stockpak II system consists of a program disk and one or more database disks, depending on your choice of subscription. Each database disk contains financial information on up to 1,500 companies. Database disks are updated as of the last trading day of each month and sent to subscribers, who normally receive them around the 10th day of the following month.

Annual Stockpak II subscriptions are available to four different databases. One database contains information about 1,500 stocks listed on the New York Stock Exchange, while the second covers the same number of stocks listed on the American Stock Exchange. A third includes two disks covering a total of 2,200 over-the-counter stocks. Finally, a composite database is available with information on 1,500 leading companies listed on the New York Stock Exchange, the American Stock Exchange, and over the counter.

Each Stockpak II database disk contains 83 predefined data items including: assets, balance sheet data, beta, book value per share, cash, percent change in dividend versus five years earlier, percent change in net income versus the prior year, percent change in sales versus the prior year, common shares outstanding, debt, dividend amount per share, earnings per share for the last 12 months and each of the last five years, ex-dividend date, primary stock exchange, compound annual rate of growth for earnings per share over the past five years, high and low price per share traded within the current and past year, liabilities, net income, options availability, price of the stock on the last trading day of the month and each of the last four quarters, sales for each of the last five years, volume of shares traded during the month, company's fiscal year-end, and over 40 financial ratios representing combinations of other data items. Standard & Poor's proprietary ranking for each company and earnings per share estimates are also included.

In addition to the 83 predefined data items, you can create 25 data items by combining two of the 83 existing data items. For example, you might create a new ratio that calculates a company's sales per share by entering a formula that divides the sales figure for a given period by the number of common shares outstanding.

Stockpak II is extremely fast and easy to use. This is due, in part, to the fact that the software is written in a combined programming language and operating system called FORTH instead of using the standard IBM operating systems (MS-DOS or PC-DOS). The software requires no installation procedures. You just insert the disks in the disk drives, turn the power on, and in a few seconds, the Stockpak II Main Menu appears on the screen.

From the Main Menu you can select the three main applications of Stockpak II—looking up the key financial facts on a company, graphically comparing information on companies, and performing simple or complex screening procedures to find certain types of companies.

The most powerful feature of Stockpak II is its screening capability. After you define your own screening criteria or choose one of the 10 predefined criteria sets, the program searches through the database disk for companies meeting your conditions. You can use any combination of up to seven individual criteria. A typical screening is performed in less than 30 seconds, allowing you to perform multiple screenings quickly. For example, you could screen for stocks with a yield greater than or equal to 10 percent and a market price less than or equal to $25 per share.

After screening a database, a list of the ticker symbols for the companies meeting your predefined conditions will be displayed. As shown in Exhibit 6–3, 23 stocks met the screening criteria in this example. Next, you can save the ticker symbols in a spinoff file and produce reports in 10 ready-made formats or in a format that you create yourself.

Exhibits 6–4 through 6–6 show three of the ready-made report formats. The first report lists income related data items for each of the stocks screened. The second report provides profile

---

EXHIBIT 6–3   Sample Stock Screening Using Stockpak II

```
Q
                    STOCKS FULFILLING CRITERIA SET# 14

                                                           JAN 1986


               PRICE
               -----
               PRICE LE 25.00
               YIELD% GE 10.00
```

APP	BBE	BLYVY	CEP	DQU	DTE	EDP	FMP	GAS	GOP
GSU	ICB	IPC	KLT	LOG	NMK	OEC	PE	PIN	SAX
SEQ	UMR	WHLDY							

EXHIBIT 6–4   Stockpak II Report of Income-Related Data Items

---

```
Q
PAGE 1 OF 1      REPORT: INCOME              FILE: PRICE           JAN 1986
```

STOCK	YIELD%	PAYRATIO%	DIVIDEND	EXDATE	CHGDIV%	PRICE
APP	12.50	333.00	2.10	NOV 8	0.00	16.75
BBE	18.00	0.00	1.80	NOV 22	0.00	10.00
BLYVY	14.19	51.00	0.62	DEC 20	-1.00	4.3.
CEP	15.81	0.00	1.80	OCT 21	0.00	11.38
DQU	12.69	93.00	2.06	NOV 27	17.00	16.25
DTE	10.63	73.00	1.68	NOV 29	6.00	15.88
EDP	25.38	0.00	3.30	FEB 3	0.00	13.00
FMP	13.31	0.00	2.20	DEC 24	0.00	16.50
GAS	14.13	0.00	3.04	DEC 26	22.00	21.63
GOP	25.50	452.00	1.40	JAN 6	0.00	5.50
GSU	12.63	73.00	1.64	NOV 12	20.00	13.00
ICB	10.81	0.00	2.19	DEC 20	5.00	20.25
IPC	11.13	76.00	2.64	JAN 6	15.00	23.88
KLT	10.38	49.00	2.36	NOV 22	33.00	22.63
LOG	12.50	0.00	2.60		0.00	20.75
NMK	10.13	79.00	2.08	NOV 18	37.00	20.50
OEC	11.50	77.00	1.88	DEC 2	4.00	16.38
PE	12.69	87.00	2.20	NOV 6	22.00	17.38
PIN	13.81	108.00	1.00	NOV 5	-56.00	7.25
SAX	15.50	0.00	1.20	DEC 24	0.00	7.75
SEQ	10.50	138.00	1.92	NOV 8	0.00	18.25
UMR	18.38	0.00	1.93	NOV 8	0.00	10.50
WHLDY	15.69	48.00	3.30	NOV 4	-53.00	21.00
SUMMARY	AVG	AVG	AVG		AVG	AVG
	14.25	75.52	2.04		3.09	15.25

EXHIBIT 6-5   Stockpak II Report Providing Profile Information

```
Q
PAGE 1 OF 1       REPORT: PROFILE1          FILE: PRICE          JAN 1986
```

STOCK	SPRANK	PRICE	PE	YIELD%	GROWEPS%	BOOKSHR
APP	NR	16.75	26.56	12.50	0.00	15.57
BBE	NR	10.00	0.00	18.00	0.00	9.32
BLYVY	NR	4.38	3.63	14.19	-20.00	0.00
CEP	NR	11.38	0.00	15.81	0.00	0.00
DQU	B+	16.25	7.31	12.69	3.00	16.10
DTE	A-	15.88	6.94	10.63	5.00	16.68
EDP	NR	13.00	0.00	25.38	0.00	0.00
FMP	NR	16.50	0.00	13.31	0.00	19.14
GAS	B+	21.63	0.00	14.13	-94.00	21.56
GOP	NR	5.50	17.75	25.50	0.00	1.08
GSU	A-	13.00	5.81	12.63	1.00	15.54
ICB	NR	20.25	81.00	10.81	3.00	18.72
IPC	A-	23.88	6.88	11.13	6.00	23.34
KLT	A-	22.63	4.75	10.38	11.00	25.23
LOG	NR	20.75	0.00	12.50	0.00	0.00
NMK	A	20.50	7.75	10.13	6.00	19.11
OEC	B+	16.38	6.75	11.50	9.00	15.78
PE	A-	17.38	6.81	12.69	5.00	17.70
PIN	NR	7.25	7.81	13.81	-24.00	27.29
SAX	NR	7.75	0.00	15.50	0.00	12.32
SEQ	NR	18.25	13.13	10.50	48.00	16.10
UMR	NR	10.50	0.00	18.38	0.00	0.00
WHLDY	NR	21.00	3.06	15.69	-11.00	0.00
SUMMARY		AVG	AVG	AVG	AVG	AVG
		15.25	8.95	14.25	-2.26	12.63

EXHIBIT 6-6   Stockpak II Report Showing Earnings per Share Data

```
Q
PAGE 1 OF 1       REPORT: EARNINGS1         FILE: PRICE          JAN 1986
```

STOCK	GROWEPS%	CHGEPS%	CHGEPS5%	EPS1	EPS2	EPS5
APP	0.00	-33.74	0.00	0.84	1.27	0.00
BBE	0.00	0.00	0.00	0.87	0.00	0.00
BLYVY	-20.00	-41.69	-54.51	1.89	3.24	4.16
CEP	0.00	0.00	0.00	0.00	0.00	0.00
DQU	3.00	0.35	21.46	2.21	2.20	1.82
DTE	5.00	-0.35	25.89	2.20	2.21	1.75
EDP	0.00	0.00	0.00	0.00	0.00	0.00
FMP	0.00	0.00	0.00	1.09	0.00	0.00
GAS	-94.00	-526.42	-241.25	-7.06	1.66	5.00
GOP	0.00	0.00	0.00	0.95	0.00	0.00
GSU	1.00	-0.68	12.21	2.30	2.31	2.05
ICB	3.00	0.00	0.00	0.00	0.00	0.00
IPC	6.00	5.97	40.33	4.02	3.80	2.87
KLT	11.00	7.91	54.03	4.48	4.15	2.91
LOG	0.00	0.00	0.00	2.46	0.00	0.00
NMK	6.00	2.54	52.30	2.84	2.77	1.87
OEC	9.00	12.68	64.10	2.50	2.22	1.52
PE	5.00	12.70	35.16	2.70	2.40	2.00
PIN	-24.00	-76.18	-66.91	1.06	4.46	3.21
SAX	0.00	0.00	0.00	0.00	0.00	0.00
SEQ	48.00	26.43	1.67T	1.38	1.09	0.08
UMR	0.00	0.00	0.00	0.00	0.00	0.00
WHLDY	-11.00	-38.14	-66.05	6.87	11.10	20.23
SUMMARY	AVG	AVG	AVG	AVG	AVG	AVG
	-2.26	-28.20	67.25	1.46	1.95	2.15

information for each stock. And the final report shows earnings per share information.

Unique to Stockpak II is its ability to graphically compare information on several companies. This is accomplished by choosing selection two from the Main Menu and then entering the ticker symbols and data items on which you want the comparisons based. Rather than entering the ticker symbols manually, you can have them entered from a spinoff file containing the ticker symbols for the companies that have met a particular set of screening criteria.

Two graph formats permit quick and easy comparisons. A multiple graph format allows you to display bar graphs for up to four data items and up to five companies. If you have requested a comparison of over five companies, a single bar graph will display each data item one at a time. Exhibit 6–7 shows a graphic comparison of the percent yield on the 23 stocks identified during the screening process in the example above.

Screening Stocks with Value/Screen Plus

Value Line's Value/Screen Plus software includes a program disk and one database disk. The database disk is updated monthly or quarterly depending upon your choice of subscription.

The database disk contains 37 items of information on more than 1,600 companies, which account for more than 95 percent of the stock trading activity on all U.S. stock exchanges. The 37 data items are divided into four categories: ratings and estimates, market data, historical measures, and growth projections.

The ratings and estimates category includes timeliness rank, safety rank, financial strength rating, industry code, industry rank, price stability index, beta, current earnings per share, and current dividend. The market data category consists of recent price, 12-month high price, 12-month low price, current price/earnings ratio, current yield, price/book value, 3-month percent change in price, 6-month percent change in price, market value, and options listing. In the historical measures category are sales, percent return on net worth, percent of retained to common equity, book value per share, debt as a percentage of capital, last quarter earnings per share percent change, 12-month earnings per share percent change, five-year earnings per share growth, five-year dividend growth, and five-year book value growth. The data included in growth projections are estimated percent change in earnings per

EXHIBIT 6-7   Stockpak II's Graphic Comparison of the
Percent Yield on the Stocks Screened

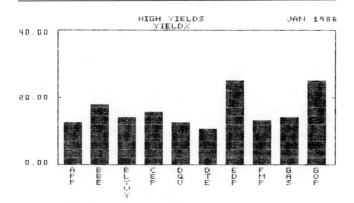

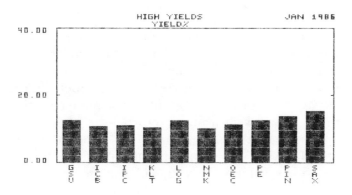

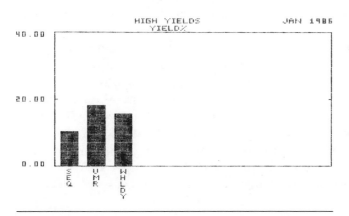

EXHIBIT 6–8 Sample Screening Using Value/Screen Plus

```
                              SCREEN DATA BASE                 Data: Dec 1985
    ----- CATEGORIES -----          --------- MARKET DATA -----------

  R Ratings & Estimates     1 Recent Price           6 Price/Book Value
  M Market Data             2 12-Month High Price     7 3-Mo % Price Change
  H Historical Measures     3 12-Month Low Price      8 6-Mo % Price Change
  G Growth Projections      4 Current P-E Ratio       9 Market Value ($mill)
                            5 Current Yield (%)       10 Options Listing


        VARIABLE              <=>        VALUE            # OF STOCKS
        Starting Stock List    =         All                1587
   1    Recent Price           <         20.00               582
   2    Current P-E Ratio      <         12                  149
   3    Timeliness Rank        <=        2                    28
   4    Safety Rank            <=        3                    11
   5
   6



  F3  S/R/D CRITERIA     F4  S/R/D LIST      F5  VIEW     F9  INSERT    F10  DELETE
```

share for the next quarter, estimated percent change in earnings per share for the quarter after the next one, estimated percent change in earnings per share for the next fiscal year, projected three- to five-year appreciation, projected earnings per share growth, projected dividend growth, projected book value growth, and projected three- to five-year average return.

Value/Screen Plus is easy to use. It uses the standard IBM operating system (PC-DOS). After basic installation procedures, you can be ready to use Value/Screen Plus in a matter of a few minutes.

The Main Menu consists of seven choices. They are installation, screen database, analysis of stock list, report on screened or saved list, report on selected tickers, portfolio management, and exit to DOS. Note that although the software's primary purpose is to screen socks, it also includes portfolio management capabilities. In addition, the software allows transfer of any of the data items to a spreadsheet program, such as Lotus 1-2-3.

Selecting the screen database choice for the Main Menu enables you to select stocks based on criteria you specify. Screening criteria can be created using any of the 37 data items.

For example, in Exhibit 6–8, four screening criteria have been selected. They are: market price less than $20 per share, current price/earnings ratio less than 12, timeliness rank less than or equal

EXHIBIT 6-9   Sample Value/Screen Plus Screening Report

```
                                     VIEW REPORT
SAMPLE REPORT
Data:   Dec 1985
                     Ticker   Recent  Current  Time-   Safety  Prj 3-5 Yr
  Company Name       Symbol   Price   Yield    liness  Rank    Apprec %
-----------------    ------   ------  -------  ------  ------  ----------
BROKEN HILL          BRKNY    11.688    4.6      2       3          84
CENTURY TEL.         CTL      12.625    6.4      2       2          39
DURIRON              DURI     12.375    4.5      2       3          62
FIRST EXECUTIVE      FEXC     17.000    0.0      2       3         121
FOX PHOTO INC.       FPI      13.750    4.9      2       3          53
GLENDALE FED         GLN      14.500    1.7      2       3         245
GRACO INC.           GRAC     19.125    2.5      1       3          70
NIKE, INC'B'         NIKE     13.500    3.0      1       3          48
RADICE CORP.         RI       15.875    0.0      1       3         120
STERLING BNCP        STL      13.625    5.9      2       3          -8
TORO CO.             TTC      18.750    2.1      2       3          73
                              -------  ------  ------  ------  ----------
        Averages              14.801    3.2     1.7     2.9         82
```

to 2, and safety rank less than or equal to 3. In the column furthest to the right the number of stocks remaining at each stage of the screening process is listed. This feature is particularly valuable, as it lets you see the effect of each screening criteria.

Once the Value/Screen Plus database has been screened to the number of stocks desired, you can generate reports that include any of the 37 data items. You select the data items you want included in the report and the report format. Reports can be shown on the screen, printed, or saved on a disk in DIF format (Data Interchange Format) for subsequent transfer to a spreadsheet program. A sample report meeting the screening criteria described above is shown in Exhibit 6–9.

If you are interested in knowing how the stocks screened compare to the total population of stocks on the data disk, you can display a statistical analysis of the Value/Screen Plus database. As illustrated in Exhibit 6–10, the statistical analysis lists each of the 37 data items along with high, low, mean, median, and standard deviation values.

COMPUSERVE: AN ON-LINE ALTERNATIVE

As an alternative to using a stock screening software package, you can screen for stocks on-line through CompuServe. CompuServe can be accessed by virtually any personal computer with a standard communications software package or by a dumb terminal with communication capabilities.

EXHIBIT 6–10   Statistical Analysis of Value/Screen Plus Database

```
      STATISTICAL ANALYSIS OF VALUE/SCREEN PLUS DATA BASE
                         Dec 1985

Variable Name            High      Low    Sample  Mean  Median  St. Dev.
---------------          ----      ---    ------  ----  ------  --------


                 ------ RATINGS & ESTIMATES ------

 1 Timeliness Rank          5        1      1516     3      3         1
 2 Safety Rank              5        1      1587     3      3         1
 3 Financial Strength     A++        C      1585    B+     B+        NA
 4 Industry Code           NA       NA      1587    NA     NA        NA
 5 Industry Rank           91        1      1568    45     47        26
 6 Price Stability        100        5      1575    52     50        29
 7 Beta                   2.00     0.40     1571  1.00   1.00      0.27
 8 Current EPS           35.96   -15.96     1585  2.20   1.99      2.49
 9 Current Dividend       7.00     0.00     1587  0.93   0.65      0.95


                 --------- MARKET DATA -----------

 1 Recent Price         279.375    0.219    1587  29.444  25.500  19.951
 2 12-Month High Price  276.500    1.375    1585  32.240  28.500  22.969
 3 12-Month Low Price   227.000    0.188    1585  21.292  18.500   8.540
 4 Current P-E Ratio      59.7      2.0     1385    14.7    12.8     8.1
 5 Current Yield (%)      17.3      0.0     1587     2.9     2.6     2.6
 6 Price/Book Value      86.11     0.10     1565    2.06    1.47    2.99
 7 3-Mo % Price Change    75.4    -70.0     1584     4.2     4.7    13.7
 8 6-Mo % Price Change   150.0    -78.1     1581     6.0     4.9    19.9
 9 Market Value ($mill) 85163.4     1.1     1587  1242.0   404.9   726.5
10 Options Listing         NA       NA      1587      NA      NA      NA


                 ------- HISTORICAL MEASURES ------

 1 Sales ($ mill)      90854.0      2.3     1465  2168.0   566.6  1784.7
 2 % Return Net Worth     55.6      0.0     1436    13.4    13.2     6.7
 3 % Retained to Com Eq   51.5      0.0     1354     9.6     9.1     6.1
 4 Book Value per Share  99.01   -19.31     1587   18.81   15.93   13.53
 5 Debt as % of Capital    .97        0     1572      30      28      20
 6 Last Qtr EPS % Chg    961.5    -98.2     1268    13.6     5.5    81.1
 7 12-Month EPS % Chg    750.0   -100.0     1323     5.8     3.7    57.0
 8 5-Yr EPS Growth        95.0    -46.0     1329     7.1     7.0    16.0
 9 5-Yr Divd Growth       80.5    -48.0     1278     9.4     9.0    13.0
10 5-Yr Book Val Growth   94.5    -47.0     1518    10.4     9.0    12.5


                 ------- GROWTH PROJECTIONS -------

 1 Est % Chg EPS Qtr 1   800.0    -98.4     1305    19.2    10.1    66.9
 2 Est % Chg EPS Qtr 2   900.0    -99.5     1321    29.4    13.3    77.4
 3 Est % Chg EPS Fis Yr  614.3    -94.9     1325    14.7     8.5    60.5
 4 Prj 3-5 Yr Apprec %     900      -38     1586      85      71      69
 5 Prj EPS Growth         98.0    -15.5     1377    15.3    13.0    11.2
 6 Prj Divd Growth        80.5    -27.5     1403     9.2     8.0     9.3
 7 Prj Book Val Growth    90.5    -38.0     1534     9.4     9.0     7.8
 8 Prj 3-5 Yr Av Return     78      -11     1584      18      17       8
```

CompuServe's security screening feature allows you to search through the 46,000 securities that are actively traded in the United States and Canada to identify those that best meet your own predefined set of criteria.

Let's look at an example (See Exhibit 6–11 for an illustration of an actual search). Suppose you want to locate all common stocks traded on the New York Stock Exchange having a market price less than or equal to $20 per share, an annual dividend greater than $2 per share, and a price/earnings ratio of less than 10.

After signing on to CompuServe, you select the Security Screening choice on the Investment Analysis menu. From the first screening menu, you select common stock for the issue type. Other available issue types include preferred stock, warrants, convertible bonds, municipal bonds, corporate bonds, mutual funds, and put and call options. Selecting common stock narrows down the population of securities to approximately 12,600 from over 46,000.

The next choice you make is the exchange from which you want the stocks screened. More than one exchange can be selected from a list of 17 exchanges. In this case, you select the New York Stock Exchange and reduce the population of securities to about 1,550 issues.

Continuing the search, you identify the specific criteria that you want to use to screen the remaining 1,550 securities. For all issue types, you can narrow down the search by industry (using SIC code) or Standard & Poor's quality rating. Stocks can be screened on indicated annual dividend, recent earnings per share, number of shares outstanding, volatility (beta coefficient), and price/earnings ratio. Debt issues can be selected by amount outstanding, maturity date, bond coupon rate, yield to maturity, or Moody's raing. Options can be screened on open interest, exercise price, or expiration date.

In addition to identifying the specific criteria, you specify the range into which you want each of the criteria to fall. In this example, you designate a market price less than or equal to $20 per share, an indicated annual dividend greater than $2, and a price/earnings ratio of less than 10.

Finally, you have narrowed the list of stocks to 16. Each of these stocks can be further researched one at a time before making a final investment decision.

EXHIBIT 6–11 Sample On-Line Stock Screening
through CompuServe

CompuServe   SCREEN

Using the following menus, you will be able to screen
through the MicroQuote database. You will continue to
narrow down your selection set until you have a final
group of issues you want to report.

              ISSUE TYPES

1 Common   9 Certificate
2 Preferred   10 Index
3 Warrant   11 Put Option
4 Conv. Bond   12 Call Option
5 Unit   13 When-issued
6 Muni Bond   14 Conv. Preferred
7 Corp. Debt   15 US Govt/Agency debt
8 Mutual Fund   16 Unassigned

Enter choices, separated by commas.

!1

12566 issues found

1 Continue search
2 Redo last search
3 Start screening over
4 Abort search (exit program)
5 Report issues found

Enter choice ! 1

              EXCHANGES

1 New York   10 OTC Mutual Funds
2 American   11 OTC Equip. Trusts
3 Phil./Boston   12 Toronto/Montreal
4 Midwest   13 US Govt.
5 Pacific   14 Foreign Bonds
6 CBOE   15 Muni $ bonds
7 OTC National   16 US savings bonds
8 OTC industrial   17 Indices
9 OTC banks/trusts

Enter choices, separated by commas.

!1

1549 issues found

1 Continue search
2 Redo last search
3 Start screening over
4 Abort search (exit program)
5 Report issues found

Enter choice ! 1

EXHIBIT 6–11 *(continued)*

```
 1 SIC Code                       12 P/E ratio
 2 Shares outstanding (000's)     13 Current yield (%)
 3 Amount outstanding (000's)     14 Yield-to-maturity
 4 Open interest (contracts)      15 Moody's rating
 5 Earnings per share             16 S&P rating
 6 Indic. Annual Dividend         17 Beta coefficient
 7 Maturity date                  18 Cash ex-dates
 8 Bond coupon rate               19 Stock ex-dates
 9 Exercise price                 20 Date of 52 week high
10 Expiration date                21 Date of 52 week low
11 Latest price


Enter choice(s), separated by commas.

!6,11,12

Indicate screening criteria for each variable

Valid expressions are:

LT n       less than value of n
LE n       less than or equal to n
GT n       greater than value of n
GE n       greater than or equal to n
EQ n       equal to n

NE n       not equal to n

The symbols <  <=  >  >=  =  # may also be used.
To repeat this information, type HELP.

Valid expressions for Indic. Annual Dividend require
     numeric values.  Example:  GT 4

Indic. Annual Dividend   : GT 2

Valid expressions for Latest price require
     numeric values.  Example:  GT 4

Latest price   : LE 20

Valid expressions for P/E ratio require
     numeric values.  Example:  GT 4

P/E ratio   : LT 10

Indicate logic for multiple criteria:

1 All criteria must be met (AND logic)
2 Issues selected if any criterion met (OR logic)

Enter choice ! 1

16 issues found

1  Continue search
2  Redo last search
3  Start screening over
4  Abort search (exit program)
5  Report issues found

Enter choice ! 5

You have    16 issues selected.
Producing a report now will cost:     $4.00
What would you like to do?

1  Product a report
2  Continue the search

Enter choice ! 1
```

EXHIBIT 6–11 (*concluded*)

```
Available report formats are:

1 Cusip Ticker Exchange Issuer/Issue Last-Price PE-Ratio Yield Beta
2 Cusip Ticker Exchange Issuer/Issue Last-Price
3 Ticker Exchange Last-Price EPS IAD PE-Ratio Yield Beta
4 Ticker Exchange Last-Price

Enter choice !3

Enter report filename or <CR> for terminal output:

Enter title (maximum 3 lines; <CR> when done)
Title line 1 : SAMPLE STOCK SCREENING
Title line 2 :
```

```
7-Feb-86                                                        Page:   1
                          SAMPLE STOCK SCREENING

Ticker Exc Issuer                          Price    EPS    IAD   PER   Yield Beta
------ --- ------------------------------- -----   ----   ----  ----  ------ ----
AHR     N  AMERICANA HOTELS & RLTY CORP    10.750   2.44   2.20  4.41  20.47 0.19
BHL     N  BUNKER HILL INCOME SECS INC     19.500   0.00   2.16  0.00  11.08 0.13
DSP     N  DIAMOND SHAMROCK OFFSHORE PA    17.125   0.00   2.80  0.00  16.35-1.00
DQU     N  DUQUESNE LT CO                  17.625   2.26   2.06  7.80  11.69 0.47
EED     N  ENTEX ENERGY DEV LTD            10.750   0.00   2.50  0.00  23.26-1.00
EP      N  ENSERCH EXPL PARTNERS LTD       16.500   1.81   2.40  9.12  14.55-1.00
FMP     N  FREEPORT MCMORAN ENERGY         15.875   0.00   2.20  0.00  13.86-1.00
KEP     N  KANEB ENERGY PARTNERS LTD       12.500   0.00   2.40  0.00  19.20-1.00
LRT     N  LL & E RTY TR                    8.750   2.25   2.26  3.89  25.83 0.21
NIP     N  NEWHALL INVT PPTYS              16.500   3.26   2.77  5.06  16.79 0.04
NET     N  NORTH EUROPEAN OIL RTY TR       15.875   2.01   2.02  7.90  12.72 0.19
PE      N  PHILADELPHIA ELEC CO            19.625   2.56   2.20  7.67  11.21 0.66
SBR     N  SABINE RTY TR                   12.375   2.39   2.29  5.18  18.51 0.06
SLP     N  SUN ENERGY PARTNERS L P         20.000   0.00   2.90  0.00  14.50-1.00

Press <CR> for more !
```

```
7-Feb-86                                                        Page:   2
                          SAMPLE STOCK SCREENING

Ticker Exc Issuer                          Price    EPS    IAD   PER   Yield Beta
------ --- ------------------------------- -----   ----   ----  ----  ------ ----
EXP     N  TRANSCO EXPL PARTNERS LTD       15.750  -0.10   2.36  0.00  14.98 0.23
UXP     N  UNION EXPL PARTNERS LTD         16.875   0.00   2.49  0.00  14.76-1.00

Last page !
```

SOURCE: By permission of CompuServe, Inc.

CONCLUSION

Individual and professional investors alike can benefit from using the stock screening capabilities of a software package or on-line service. Utilizing the full potential of the personal computer, they quickly manipulate large quantities of financial information. They can save you hours, and maybe days, of time and help you focus on the stocks with potential to meet your individual investment objectives.

CHAPTER 7

Analyzing Individual Companies

In Chapter 6, we looked at stock screening software and how it can be used to arrive at a list of just the stocks that interest you. Normally, that list will contain 10 to 25 stocks that will have to be researched further before you can make a final investment decision.

This chapter focuses on analyzing individual companies that you have identified through the stock screening process or otherwise. It illustrates additional capabilities of Stockpak II and Value/Screen Plus. In addition, it demonstrates the value of software such as The Evaluation Form, a package that utilizes a fundamentalist approach to investing that has been in constant use for over 30 years.

LOOKING UP INFORMATION WITH STOCKPAK II

In addition to the stock screening capabilities of Standard & Poor's Stockpak II described in the previous chapter, you can quickly look up information on any one of the hundreds of companies on the data disk. You simply choose selection one from Stockpak II's Main Menu and enter the ticker symbol of the company for which you want information. Stockpak II presents you with three display pages containing 83 predefined data items plus up to 16 user created ratios.

The first display page contains general characteristics of the company, earnings per share performance, annual sales information, stock price performance, dividend information, and balance sheet items (see Exhibit 7–1). The second display page lists a variety of performance ratios (see Exhibit 7–2). The ratios are

EXHIBIT 7–1 Stockpak II's Lookup Data for IBM

Q

IBM	LOOKUP DATA		JAN 1986
SP500	YES	PRICE	155.50
SPRANK	A+	VOLUME	28.48M
OPTIONS	YES	PRICEQ1	127.00
YREND	DEC	PRICEQ2	123.75
INDGRP	4201	PRICEQ3	123.88
EXCHG	NYS	PRICEQ4	123.13
COMSHRS	614.86M	HIGH	158.75
EPSEST	10.75	LOW	99.00
EPS12	9.86	BETA	0.77
EPS1	10.77		
EPS2	9.04	DIVIDEND	4.40
EPS3	7.39	CHGDIV%	19.00
EPS4	5.63	EXDATE	NOV 6
EPS5	5.72	NET	6.58B
GROWEPS%	14.00	CHGNET%	20.00
		BOOKSHR	47.73
SALES1	45.94B	CASH	3.67B
SALES2	40.18B	ASSETS	22.95B
SALES3	34.36B	LIABS	10.15B
SALES4	29.07B	DEBT	3.68B
SALES5	26.21B	BALSHEET	SEP 85
CHGSALES%	14.00	FOOTNOTE	NONE

EXHIBIT 7–2 Stockpak II's Lookup Ratios for IBM

Q

IBM	LOOKUP RATIOS		JAN 1986
BELOWHIGH%	2.05	MKTVAL	95.61B
BOOKVAL	29.35B	NASSTSPR%	9.54
CASHASSTS%	15.98	NETASSTS	9.12B
CASHLIABS%	36.14	NETASSTSHR	14.83
CASHPRICE%	3.84	PAYRATIO%	45.00
CASHSHR	5.97	PE	15.75
CHGEPS%	19.19	PRICEBOOK%	325.00
CHGEPS5%	88.39	RETBOOK%	20.63
CURRATIO	2.26	RETSALES%	14.00
DEBTBOOK%	12.55	TOTALCAP	33.03B
DEBTCAP%	11.15	WKGCAP	12.80B
DIFFEPS	1.73	WKGCAPPR%	13.39
DIFFEPS5	5.05	WKGCAPSHR	20.82
DIFFHIGH	3.25	YIELD%	2.81

arranged in alphabetical order. The final display page shows two bar charts (see Exhibit 7–3). One compares the earnings per share for each of the last five years with the estimated earnings per share. The other charts sales for each of the last five years side by side.

EXHIBIT 7–3 Stockpak II's Earnings per Share and Sales Charts for IBM

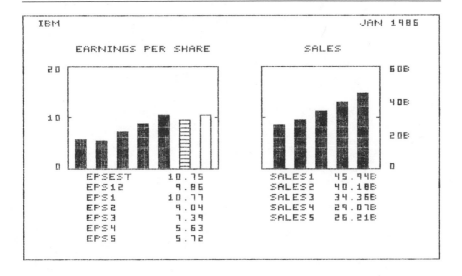

EXHIBIT 7–4 Stockpak II's Comparison Graphics for Five Companies

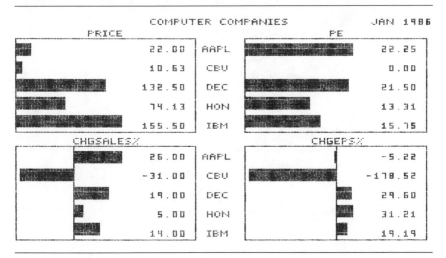

One final feature of Stockpak II is worth noting. It has the unique capability to graphically compare data items of your choice for several stocks at a time. For example, in Exhibit 7–4 a comparison of the market price, price/earnings ratio, percent change in sales, and percent change in earnings per share is provided for

---

EXHIBIT 7–5 Value/Screen Plus Ticker Report for IBM

```
                VALUE/SCREEN PLUS TICKER REPORT


IBM                     IBM      Data:    Dec 1985



            ------ RATINGS & ESTIMATES ------


Timeliness Rank          2     Price Stability          95
Safety Rank              1     Beta                   1.05
Financial Strength     A++     Current EPS           11.24
Industry Code         3573     Current Dividend       4.40
Industry Rank           78


            ---------- MARKET DATA -------------


Recent Price        139.000    Price/Book Value         3.22
12-Month High Price 138.250    3-Mo % Price Change       9.8
12-Month Low Price  116.000    6-Mo % Price Change       8.1
Current P-E Ratio      12.4    Market Value ($mill) 85163.4
Current Yield (%)       3.2    Options Listing          CBOE


            ------ HISTORICAL MEASURES ------


Sales ($ mill)      45937.0    Last Qtr EPS % Chg       -7.7
% Return Net Worth      24.8    12-Month EPS % Chg       -4.1
% Retained to Com Eq    15.4    5-Yr EPS Growth         12.5
Book Value per Share   43.23    5-Yr Divd Growth         5.0
Debt as % of Capital     11    5-Yr Book Val Growth     10.5


            ------ GROWTH PROJECTIONS --------


Est % Chg EPS Qtr 1     22.3    Prj EPS Growth          13.0
Est % Chg EPS Qtr 2     36.6    Prj Divd Growth         12.5
Est % Chg EPS Fis Yr    -1.1    Prj Book Val Growth     13.5
Prj 3-5 Yr Apprec %       76    Prj 3-5 Yr Av Return      18
```

---

five computer companies. By having key data graphed side by side for companies, you can easily compare information important to making an investment decision.

REPORT ON SELECTED TICKER SYMBOL WITH VALUE/SCREEN PLUS

Like Stockpak II, Value Line's Value Screen Plus allows you to look up information on specific companies, in addition to its stock screening capabilities. You simply enter a stock's ticker symbol and, as illustrated in Exhibit 7–5 for IBM, a report containing the 37 data items in the Value/Screen Plus database are listed. In

EXHIBIT 7–6   Value/Screen Plus Comparison Report for Five Companies

VALUE/SCREEN PLUS COMPARISON REPORT
Data: Dec 1985

	APPLE COMPUTER	COMMODORE INT'L	DIGITAL EQPMNT	HONEYWELL INC.	IBM
Timeliness Rank	4	5	3	4	2
Safety Rank	3	5	3	2	1
Financial Strength	B++	C+	A++	A+	A++
Industry Code	3573	3573	3573	3573	3573
Industry Rank	78	78	78	78	78
Price Stability	5	5	45	65	95
Beta	1.70	1.50	1.25	1.20	1.05
Current EPS	0.98	-4.74	6.41	6.20	11.24
Current Dividend	0.00	0.00	0.00	2.00	4.40
Recent Price	19.375	10.750	118.500	68.000	139.000
12-Month High Price	31.125	27.625	125.625	67.375	138.250
12-Month Low Price	14.250	8.250	85.250	54.250	116.000
Current P-E Ratio	19.8	NA	18.5	11.0	12.4
Current Yield (%)	0.0	0.0	0.0	2.9	3.2
Price/Book Value	2.53	1.52	1.54	1.33	3.22
3-Mo % Price Change	29.2	7.5	13.3	10.3	9.8
6-Mo % Price Change	11.5	6.2	13.5	13.1	8.1
Market Value ($mill)	1172.9	337.8	7021.5	3176.5	85163.4
Options Listing	None	Phila	Amex	CBOE	CBOE
Sales ($ mill)	1515.9	883.1	6686.3	6073.6	45937.0
% Return Net Worth	12.7	NA	8.4	12.4	24.8
% Retained to Com Eq	12.7	NA	8.4	8.6	15.4
Book Value per Share	7.67	7.08	76.87	50.97	43.23
Debt as % of Capital	0	13	16	22	11
Last Qtr EPS % Chg	-14.3	NA	-13.0	-3.1	-7.7
12-Month EPS % Chg	2.1	NA	-9.4	-3.2	-4.1
5-Yr EPS Growth	71.0	35.5	6.0	3.0	12.5
5-Yr Divd Growth	NA	NA	NA	12.0	5.0
5-Yr Book Val Growth	NA	59.0	19.0	8.5	10.5
Est % Chg EPS Qtr 1	-33.3	150.0	-8.8	11.5	22.3
Est % Chg EPS Qtr 2	87.5	NA	25.0	20.0	36.6
Est % Chg EPS Fis Yr	61.6	NA	13.8	-4.6	-1.1
Prj 3-5 Yr Apprec %	158	179	126	47	76
Prj EPS Growth	18.0	0.5	24.0	11.0	13.0
Prj Divd Growth	0.0	0.0	NA	8.5	12.5
Prj Book Val Growth	19.0	11.0	12.5	8.5	13.5
Prj 3-5 Yr Av Return	27	29	23	13	18

addition, a comparison report can be prepared which shows all 37 data items for several stocks side by side as illustrated in Exhibit 7–6.

SPECIFIC FUNDAMENTALIST APPROACHES

In addition to the stock screening packages, some fundamental analysis software packages employ a specific fundamental approach to investing. To give you an idea of how you can analyze

EXHIBIT 7–7 The Evaluation Form's Library Form

```
                        LIBRARY FORM VERS 3.0
================================================================
                              DATA BELOW RELATES TO COLUMNS 1 TO 0
  COMPANY NAME............
  EXCHANGE................      1:  YEAR
  TICKER SYMBOL...........      2:  NET BEFORE TAXES   (S&P ONLY)
  DJIA....................      3:  SALES OR REVENUES  ($MILL)
  TODAY's DATE............      4:  EARNINGS PER SHARE
  LAST FULL YR. OF DATA...      5:  BOOK VALUE  (PER SHARE)
  DATA OF PUBLISHED DATA..      6:  YEARLY HIGH PRICE
  S)& P or V)ALU-LINE?....      7:  YEARLY LOW PRICE
  S & P RATING............      8:  DIVIDENDS PAID (PER SHARE)
  V-L TIMELINESS RATING...      9:  INCOME TAX RATE IN % (V-L ONLY)
  V-L SAFETY RATING.......      0:  NET PROFIT ($MILL)  (V-L ONLY)
  EPS EST (OUTSIDE SOURCE)
```

1	2	3	4	5	6	7	8	9	0
19									
19									
19									
19									
19									
19									

```
  PRESENT PRICE..........    | LATEST QUARTER EPS............
  HIGH PRICE THIS YEAR...    | YEAR AGO QUARTER EPS..........
  LOW PRICE THIS YEAR....    | # OF SHARES OUTSTANDING (MILL)
  CURRENT P/E RATIO......    | SELECTED TAX RATE IN % (S & P)
  CURRENT DIV. (YR)......    | PREPARED BY:
```

individual companies with these packages, let's examine one, The Evaluation Form from Investor's Software.

The Evaluation Form allows you to examine one company at a time using a fundamentalist approach developed in 1951 by the National Association of Investors Corporation (NAIC) of Royal Oaks, Michigan. NAIC members have been doing better than the stock market averages since then.

The method used by The Evaluation Form is easy to understand. It manipulates about 60 elements of financial data for a company and presents results in a way that makes stock selection easy.

To enter data, you fill in the blanks on a data entry sheet (see Exhibit 7–7). The information required for the form is taken from a Standard & Poor's Sheet or the *Value Line Investment Survey*, both readily available at libraries and stock brokerage houses. In less than 10 minutes, you can enter all of the required data. Once this is done, the program calculates approximately 50 values, including buy, hold, and sell price ranges for each stock. Printed results are provided on two pages as illustrated in Exhibits 7–8 and 7–9.

EXHIBIT 7–8   Page 1 of The Evaluation Form's Report for IBM

```
===================================================================================
!! EVALUATION FORM 3.0    !!     FOR MOST      !! P.O. BOX 'N'            !!
!! COPYRIGHT 1982,1986    !!  SMALL-BUSINESS   !! BRADENTON BEACH,        !!
!! INVESTOR'S SOFTWARE    !!    COMPUTERS      !! FLORIDA,     33510      !!
===================================================================================
IBM                          DATE OF STUDY         DOW JONES IND AVG 1713
EXCHANGE: NYSE
02/27/86                                           TICKER SYMBOL: IBM
PREPARED BY: T.A. MEYERS
                     EARN    BOOK   P/S  RATIO    SALES   DIV  PRE-TAX % EARN
            PRICE    PER     VALUE  HIGH AVG      OR      PER  PROF ON ON INV
YEAR   HIGH    LOW   SH.                          REVS   SHARE SALES %  CAP.
===================================================================================
1984  128.50  99.00 10.77   43.23  1.720 1.523  ****.*  4.10  25.32   24.91
1983  134.30  92.30  9.04   38.02  2.056 1.734  ****.*  3.71  24.73   23.78
1982   98.00  55.60  7.39   33.13  1.754 1.374  ****.*  3.44  23.08   22.31
1981   71.50  48.40  5.63   30.66  1.513 1.268  ****.*  3.44  20.61   18.36
1980   72.80  50.40  6.10   28.18  1.708 1.445  ****.*  3.44  22.50   21.65
1979   80.50  61.10  5.16   25.64  2.165 1.904  ****.*  3.44  24.30   20.12
===================================================================  -----  -----
      GROWTH RATES & EPS DATA           !! 2.087 <=PRES.  AVG.=> 23.42   21.85
                                        !!=================================
Growth of 'BOOK VALUE' has been. 11.01%.!!    P/E RATIOS, YIELD, PAYBACK
Growth of 'EPS' has been........ 15.85%. !!
Growth of 'SALES' has been...... 14.98%. !! YEAR    HIGH    LOW    PCT.   %HIGH
Growth of 'DIVIDENDS' has been.. 3.57%.  !!         P/E     P/E   PAYOUT  YIELD
                                        !!
Selected GROWTH RATE (of EPS) ... 15.00%!! 1984    11.93   9.19  38.07   4.14
EPS ESTIMATE for 1989 ..........$21.66 !! 1983    14.86  10.21  41.04   4.02
PREFERRED PROCEDURE (Comparison)..$19.75 !! 1982    13.26   7.52  46.55   6.19
EPS. EST. (outside source) ......$12.65 !! 1981    12.70   8.60  61.10   7.11
================================== == !! 1980    11.93   8.26  56.39   6.83
Data Published on ......  02/07/86    !!        -----  -----  -----  -----
Data from .............. (V-L)      C !! AVG.=>  12.94   8.76  48.63   5.66
Shares outstanding (MIL)  615.0     O !! P/E==>  13.08   8.99 <=== WEIGHTED
(S&P) Rating ..........   N/A       M !!
(V-L) Timeliness Rating.  2         P !! The AVERAGE P/E is ......  10.85
(V-L) Safety Rating ....  1         A !! The PRESENT P/E is ......  12.60
High this year ........ $161.00     R !! PRES. P/E is 116.13% of AVG. P/E
Low this year ......... $117.38     I !!
Present Price ......... $155.88     S !! PAYBACK in years ........   7.33
Yearly Dividend ....... $  4.40     O !!=================================
Present P/E Ratio ..... $ 12.60     N !!    FORECASTING HIGH & LOW PRICES
Latest Quarterly EPS ... $  4.36    S !!
Yr. ago Quarterly EPS .. $  3.55      !! Avg. High P/E 12.9 Times Est. EPS
==================================== !! $21.66 = FORECAST HI PRICE $280.28
    BUY-HOLD-SELL RANGES AND RATIOS   !!
                                      !! Avg. Low P/E * Est. Low EPS 94.35
 70.24  --TO--140.25  BUY RANGE       !! Avg. Low (5 yrs.)..........  69.14
140.25  --TO--210.27  HOLD RANGE      !! Lowest Price of last 3 yrs. 55.60
210.27  --TO--280.28  CONSIDER SALE   !! Price Div. will support ... 61.88
                                      !! 75% of Yrs. High Price ...$120.75
 UPSIDE/DOWNSIDE RATIO is ..    1.45  !! 75% of Yrs. Low Price ....$ 88.03
 RELATIVE VALUE ............  116.13  !!
 PRESENT PSR ...............    2.087 !! FORECAST LOW PRICE ......$ 70.24
 PRICE AT 1 to 1 RATIO .....  175.26  !!
===================================================================================
NOTE:  This material incorporates principles and procedures from The National
Association of Investors Corp's.  INVESTORS  MANUAL, 1515 E. Eleven Mile Road,
Royal Oak, Michigan  48068.  This data is assumed to be accurate but is NOT
guaranteed.  Publication of this form is for educational purposes and does
not constitute any BUY-SELL-HOLD RECOMMENDATIONS.
```

EXHIBIT 7–9   Page 2 of The Evaluation Form's Report for IBM

```
02/27/86                                    IBM

The Present Yield is .................................................   2.82%
The Average Yield over the next five years will be .................   5.06%
Yearly-Return-Low, (Projected growth of EPS) + (Average Yield) .....  20.06%
Yearly-Return-High, (Pres. Price grows to Forecast Hi) + (Avg. Yld.) 17.51%
Most recent Quarterly Earnings are up by at least 10% .............. TRUE
Growth of SALES is at least as rapid as growth of EPS ............. FALSE
Percent Pre-Tax Profit on Sales -- (Growth trend is upwards) ....... TRUE
Percent Earned on Invested Capital -- (Growth trend is upwards) .... TRUE
Growth of SALES and EARNINGS is steadily higher each year ......... FALSE
The UPSIDE/DOWNSIDE RATIO is at least 3 to 1 ...................... FALSE
Today's P/E is lower than the Average P/E ........................ FALSE
Growth of EARNINGS is above 7% ................................... TRUE
Present Price is in the BUY RANGE ................................ FALSE
All P/E ratio's are below 20 ..................................... TRUE
PRESENT P/E is in HISTORICAL RANGE ............................... TRUE
PRESENT PSR is in HISTORICAL RANGE .............................. TRUE
RELATIVE VALUE is between 90 and 110 ............................ FALSE

NOTES:
```

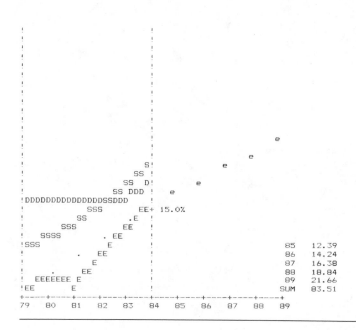

```
                                              e
                                          e
                        S!              e
                       SS !
                       SS  D!         e
                       SS DDD !    e
       !DDDDDDDDDDDDDDDDDSSDDD    !
       !          SSS        EE+ 15.0%
       !         SS        .E  !
       !      SSS         EE   !
       !   SSSS        .  EE   !
       !SSS          E       !              85   12.39
       !         .  EE       !              86   14.24
       !           E         !              87   16.38
       !       .  EE         !              88   18.84
       !  EEEEEEE E          !              89   21.66
       !EE        E          !             SUM   83.51
       +----+----+----+----+----+----+----+----+----+----+
        79   80   81   82   83   84   85   86   87   88   89
```

The hard job is to correctly interpret the results of The Evaluation Form. Fortunately, a large section of the user's manual is devoted to interpretation of which stocks to buy.

Fundamental analysis software packages like The Evaluation Form that employ a specific, time-proven approach to investing can be excellent aids. They can significantly reduce the time it takes to examine individual companies and, therefore, enable you to look at more companies.

CONCLUSION

Obtaining and analyzing key company information is essential to making good investment decisions based on a fundamental approach to the stock market. With fundamental analysis software, you can take advantage of the capabilities of the personal computer and minimize the time and effort required to employ such fundamental analysis techniques.

CHAPTER 8

Retrieving Company Information from On-Line Services

Through on-line services, investors now have instant access to current and historical quotes, up-to-the-minute news, detailed company statistics, and a wealth of other information. Three on-line services are particularly valuable for obtaining information on specific companies. They are Schwab's Investor Information Service, Dow Jones News/Retrieval, and CompuServe.

SCHWAB'S INVESTOR INFORMATION SERVICE

Charles Schwab & Co., Inc., the nation's largest discount broker, offers the capability to enter buy and sell orders and maintain portfolio information on-line. Schwab's software package called The Equalizer acts as a gateway to some of the best on-line investment research facilities available to the individual investor. Using The Equalizer, you can access information from Dow Jones News/Retrieval, Standard & Poor's, Warner Computer Systems, and Lynch, Jones & Ryan.

Schwab's Full Report is perhaps the best all-in-one company report that can be generated via an on-line service. The Full Report feature of The Equalizer retrieves information and formats it into a four-page report for the company of your choice. As illustrated in Exhibit 8–1, this report includes a description of the company; its current outlook; valuation, financial, profitability and growth statistics; balance sheet and income statement information; earnings per share forecasts; and a 52-week price and volume bar chart.

EXHIBIT 8-1 Schwab's Full Report for Apple Computer

```
                    Company Profile Report

                         02/07/86

APPLE COMPUTER INC                    Ticker Symbol:  AAPL (OTC)
                                        Last Price:   24 1/8
                                        Price Date:   02/06/86
                                        P/E Ratio:    20.96*
                                      1985 Div Yield:    .00
```

Standard & Poor's Company Description

    Apple Computer ---------------------(S&P) 28-Jan-86 Sym AAPL

Major producer of personal computers... Apple II sold mainly to
home market... Macintosh directed at office market... Earnings
to improve in FY 86, despite flat or lower revenues & sharply
higher R&D spending... 1st quarter FY 86 EPS at record levels
despite lower sales... Substantially lowered cost structure via
consolidations & layoffs... Some 25% closely held.

Outlook: FY 86 (Sep.) EPS under review... vs. FY 85's $0.99...
Cash dividends not anticipated. Tel.# 408-996-1010

Valuation   Financial

Price/Sales Ratio   .85* Price/Earnings Ratio   20.96*
Book Value per Share   8.90 Current Ratio   2.78
Price/Book Ratio   2.71 Debt/Equity Ratio   .00
Ind. Annual Dividend   NA Outstanding Shares   61,849,991
Ind. Annual Yield(%)   NA Market Value   1,492,131,033
Rel. 25-Week Price   1.33 Option Cycle Month   January

Profitability   Growth   1981-85 1984-85

Profit Margin(%)   4.11* Sales Growth(%)   54.72   26.55
Return on Equity(%)   13.18 Net Income Growth(%) 11.63   -4.42
                               Earnings Growth(%)   9.05   -5.72
                               Dividend Growth(%)   NA   NA

Summary of Balance Sheet (Thousand $)

                  1984   1985   1984   1985

Cash & Equiv   114,888 337,013 Curr. Liabilities 255,184 295,425
Current Assets 687,551 822,065 Long Term Debt   0   0
Total Assets   788,786 936,177 Total Liabilities 324,221 385,690
                                 Sharehold Equity 464,565 550,487

* Preliminary data
```
```

EXHIBIT 8–1 *(continued)*

APPLE COMPUTER INC   Page 2

52-Week Price Chart

Hi-Lo Range with Closing

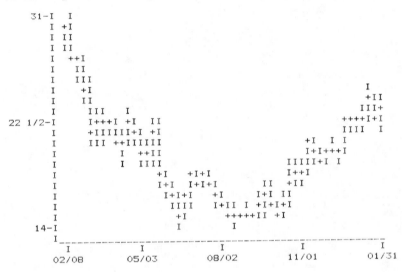

```
       31-I   I
          I  +I
          I  II
          I  II
          I  ++I
          I   II
          I   III
          I   +I                                            I
          I   II                                          +II
          I     III  I                                    III+
     22 1/2-I   I+++I +I   II                          ++++I+I
          I    +IIIIII+I +I                            IIII   I
          I    III ++IIIIII                        +I   I I
          I      I  ++II                           I+I+++I
          I      I  IIII                         IIIII+I I
          I            +I    +I+I                  I++I
          I           I+I  I+I+I          II   +II
          I           I+I+I   +I        I+I II
          I            IIII    I+II  I +I+I+I
          I            +I        ++++++II +I
       14-I            I           I
          I_____
          I        I           I           I           I        I
         02/08    05/03       08/02       11/01       01/31
```

52-Week Volume Chart

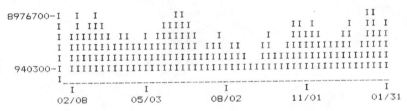

```
  8976700-I  I  I            II                        II
         I  I III          IIIII              II I    I  II I
         I IIIIIII II  I IIIIIII     I      I   IIIII  II IIII
         I IIIIIIIIIIIIIIIIIIIIIII III II   II IIIIIIIIIII IIIII
         I IIIIIIIIIIIIIIIIIIIIIIIIIIIIIIIII IIIIIIIIIIIIIIIIIIIIIII
   940300-I IIIIIIIIIIIIIIIIIIIIIIIIIIIIIIIIIIIIIIIIIIIIIIIIIIIIIIIIIII
         I_____
         I        I           I           I           I        I
        02/08    05/03       08/02       11/01       01/31
```

EXHIBIT 8–1 *(continued)*

```
APPLE COMPUTER INC                                      Page 3

Quarterly Data (Thousand $)

Quarter Ending    Mar '85   Jun '85   Sep '85   Dec '85

Sales             435,344   374,929   409,709   533,889*
Net Income          9,977   -17,209    22,357    56,925*
Profit Margin(%)     2.29     -4.59      5.46     10.66*
Earnings/Share        .16      -.28       .36       .91*
Dividend/Share        .00       .00       .00       .00*


Annual Data (Thousand $)

Year Ending Sep      1981      1982      1983      1984      1985

Sales             334,783   583,061   982,769 1,515,875 1,918,278
Change(%)                      74.2      68.6      54.2      26.5

Net Income         39,420    61,306    76,714    64,055    61,223
Change(%)                      55.5      25.1     -16.5      -4.4

Profit Margin(%)    11.77     10.51      7.81      4.23      3.19

Earnings/Share        .70      1.06      1.28      1.05       .99
Change(%)                      51.4      20.8     -18.0      -5.7

Dividend/Share        .00       .00       .00       .00       .00


Estimated Data

Year Ending Sep      1985   1986(E)   1987(E)

Earnings/Share        .99      1.78      1.89
Change(%)                      79.8       6.2

Number of Est.                   28         5


Standard & Poor's Business Summary

   Apple Computer -------------------(S&P) 10-Dec-85  Sym AAPL

Apple Computer designs, produces, and services
microprocessor-based personal computers and related software and
peripheral products, primarily for the business, education and
home markets. Its operating systems are proprietary.
The company's major revenue generator is its older Apple II
product line. Introduced in 1983, the Apple IIe with 64K of
internal memory is the second successor to the original Apple
II, introduced in 1977. The Apple IIe Professional System
includes a IIe, a display monitor, two disk drives and an

* Preliminary data
```

EXHIBIT 8–1 (concluded)

APPLE COMPUTER INC   Page 4

extended 80-column card that expands the IIe's memory to 128K.
The Apple IIc, a 7 1/2 lb. portable computer with 128K of
internal memory and a built in disk drive was introduced in May
1984. The Apple II family has a large customer base in the
education, home and small business markets.
In early 1984, Apple introduced the Macintosh, a 128K machine
incorporating integrated windowing software, which allows a user
to switch back and fourth between various applications, a
hand-held "mouse," which allows the user to enter commands
without touching the keyboard, and "icons" or pictorial
representations of functions such as a notepad, file or
wastebasket, which the user activates by pointing to them with
the mouse. A version with 512K of memory became available in
September, 1984. In January, 1985, Apple introduced its
AppleTalk local area network, which links as many as 32
computers and peripheral devices, and the LaserWriter, a high
resolution laser printer. The new products were designed to make
the Macintosh more attractive in the office environment.
In October, 1985, the company announced a major change in
strategy; it would introduce software products that would allow
the Macintosh to operate as a node on networks using
International Business Machines' communications standards, as
well as in office automation systems using Digital Equipment
Corp. products.
Foreign operations contributed 22% of revenues in fiscal 1984
and 49% of operating profit.
Employees: 4,600.

Sources of Data

The information contained herein is provided by the following
sources: Standard & Poors Corp. (Company Description and Business
Summary); Standard & Poors Compustat (Valuation, Financial,
Profitability, Growth, Summary of Balance Sheet, Annual and
Quarterly Data); Warner Computer Systems (52-week Price and
Volume Chart); and Lynch Jones and Ryan (Estimated Data).

Disclaimer

The information does not constitute representation by Charles
Schwab & Co. nor a solicitation for the purchase or sale of any
securities, nor advice regarding any investment decision.
Charles Schwab & Co. is providing access via software to the
information provided by the sources named above for discretionary
use by the software owner.

Information provided by S&P and S&P Compustat has been obtained
from sources believed to be reliable, but its accuracy and
completeness are not guaranteed.   Reproduction or redistribution
in any form is prohibited except with written permission from S&P.

SOURCE: **By permission of Charles Schwab & Co., Inc.**

To obtain a Full Report, you simply enter the ticker symbol of the company you're interested in. The Equalizer will then automatically sign on to the appropriate on-line databases, obtain the necessary information, and sign off. At that point, you have several options for displaying the report, such as a linear or semilog format for the 52-week price chart.

The cost for each Full Report is a bargain at $3.50 plus network charges. The cost of using a telecommunications network is normally less than $1 per report. In a matter of a few minutes and for a total cost of approximately $4.50, you obtain an excellent profile on a company of your choice.

The Equalizer's research function can also access Standard & Poor's Marketscope®. Marketscope provides you with constantly updated information on over 4,600 corporations including Standard & Poor's analyses of stocks and industry developments and exclusive recommendations for specific investment and portfolio objectives; commentary on current market activity, economic developments, and volatile issues; and specific Standard & Poor's earnings and dividend forecasts on over 1,000 companies.

DOW JONES NEWS/RETRIEVAL

Dow Jones & Company, Inc., the publisher of *The Wall Street Journal,* has a worldwide reputation as a leading supplier of financial information. Likewise, Dow Jones News/Retrieval (DJNR) is recognized as a premier interactive information service for investors. While other on-line services give you bits and pieces of financial information, DJNR is a complete, well-rounded on-line service for the investor.

Through DJNR, you have access to numerous proprietary and nonproprietary databases. Information sources include Dow Jones's own *Wall Street Journal, Barron's,* and the Dow Jones News Service, as well as unrelated sources such as Standard & Poor's and Media General Financial Services. Exhibit 8–2 provides a summary of the 35 databases available on DJNR.

The 35 databases are grouped into three primary categories, Business and Investor Services, General Services, and Using News/Retrieval. The Business and Investor Services category is further divided into three sections—Company/Industry Data and News, Quotes and Market Averages, and Brokerage.

DJNR is completely menu driven and very easy to use. To access a given database, you type two slashes (//) and the appro-

EXHIBIT 8-2 Summary of Dow Jones News/Retrieval Databases

DOW JONES NEWS/RETRIEVAL DATABASES

BUSINESS AND INVESTOR SERVICES

COMPANY/INDUSTRY DATA AND NEWS

//DEFINE	The Words of Wall Street
//DJNEWS	Dow Jones News
//DSCLO	Disclosure II
//EARN	Corporate Earnings Estimator
//INVEST	Investext
//KYODO	Japan Economic Daily
//MEDGEN	Media General Financial Services
//MMS	Economic and Foreign Exchange Survey
//SP	Standard & Poor's Online
//TEXT	Text-Search
//UPDATE	Weekly Economic Update
//WSJ	The Wall Street Journal Highlights Online
//WSW	Wall Street Week Online

QUOTES AND MARKET AVERAGES

//CQE	Enhanced Current Quotes
//DJA	Historical Dow Jones Averages
//FUTURES	Dow Jones Futures Quotes
//HQ	Dow Jones Historical Quotes
//RTQ	Real-Time Quotes
//TRACK	Dow Jones Tracking Service

BROKERAGE

//FIDELITY	Fidelity Investor's Express

GENERAL SERVICES

WORLD NEWS, SPORTS AND WEATHER

//NEWS	News/Retrieval World Report
//SPORTS	News/Retrieval Sports Report
//WTHR	News/Retrieval Weather Report

SHOPPING, TRAVEL AND MAIL

//AXP	American Express Advance
//MCI	MCI Mail
//STORE	Comp-u-store Online
//OAG	Official Airline Guide

EDUCATION AND ENTERTAINMENT

//ENCYC	Academic American Encyclopedia
//MEDX	Medical and Drug Reference
//MOVIES	Cineman Movie Reviews
//SCHOOL	Peterson's College Selection Service

USING NEWS/RETRIEVAL

GETTING STARTED

//DJHELP	System-wide Help
//INTRO	Intro
//MENU	Master Menu

SYMBOLS

//SYMBOL	News/Retrieval Symbols Dire

SOURCE: By permission of Dow Jones News/Retrieval.

priate mnemonic and press the enter key on your personal computer. For example, to access the Dow Jones News database, you type //DJNEWS and press the enter key.

You can easily switch to another database by typing the mnemonic command for the database you want and pressing the enter key. For example, if you are in the Dow Jones News database (//DJNEWS) and you want to go to the Corporate Earnings Estimator database, you type //EARN and press the enter key.

Ten DJNR databases are useful for retrieving information on specific companies. They are the Dow Jones News, Text-Search, Enhanced Current Quotes, Real-Time Quotes, Dow Jones Historical Quotes, Standard & Poor's Online, Media General Financial Services, Disclosure II, Corporate Earnings Estimator, and Investext databases.

The News/Retrieval Symbols Directory can be used to quickly look up a company's stock symbol, which is often required in order to obtain news, quotes and other information from DJNR databases.

Dow Jones News

The Dow Jones News database is the core of DJNR. Through this database, you can access news stories and special features from *The Wall Street Journal* and *Barron's* and also up-to-the-minute news from the Dow Jones News Service. This key information is as current as 90 seconds and goes as far back as 90 days. It is not available on any other on-line service.

You can search for the news you want by company, industry or government category. For company news, you type a period, followed by a company's stock symbol, a space, and 01, and then press the enter key to retrieve the first page of headlines for a particular company. Exhibit 8–3 shows the first page of headlines for IBM obtained by typing .IBM 01 and pressing the enter key. Subsequent pages of headlines can be examined by pressing the space bar.

If you want to view the complete text for a given headline, you simply enter the two-letter code to the left of the headline in which you are interested and press the enter key. For example, to read the complete text for the headline "IBM Waives Right to Seat on Intel Corp. Board" in Exhibit 8–3, simply type DY and press the enter key.

EXHIBIT 8–3 Company News Headlines
for IBM

```
//DJNEWS

              DOW JONES NEWS

ENTER A PERIOD (.) FOLLOWED BY A STOCK
SYMBOL OR NEWS/RETRIEVAL CATEGORY
CODE FOUND IN //SYMBOL.

      ENTER    .AAPL 01

      FOR      THE FIRST PAGE OF COMPANY
               HEADLINES ABOUT APPLE

ENTER REQUEST OR SEE //DJNEWS HELP.
    .IBM 01

  N   IBM        01/10
ED 02/07 MCDONNELL DOUGLAS GETS $289.6
  (NR) MILLION IN DEFENSE CONTRACTS
EC 02/07 IBM TO JOIN GROUP SEEKING
  (WJ) EQUIPMENT STANDARDIZATION
EB 02/07 IBM ISSUES $300 MILLION OF
  (DJ) 10-YEAR 6 3/8% EUROBONDS
EA 02/05 UAL INC SELECTS IBM TO
  (DW) DEVELOP TRAVEL AGENCY COMPUTER
DZ 02/05 IBM TO DISTRIBUTE JAVELIN
  (DJ) BUSINESS SOFTWARE
DY 02/04 IBM WAIVES RIGHT TO SEAT
  (DW) ON INTEL CORP. BOARD
DX 02/04 IBM UNVEILS NEW RELEASE
  (DJ) OF DATABASE 2 PROGRAM
DW 02/04 HEARD ON STREET: ANALYSTS SEE
  (WJ) CRAY FACING COMPETITION -3-
DV 02/04 HEARD ON STREET: ANALYSTS SEE
  (WJ) CRAY FACING COMPETITION -2-
DU 02/04 HEARD ON STREET: ANALYSTS SEE
  (WJ) CRAY FACING MORE COMPETITION
DT 01/31 HEARD ON STREET: SOME EXPERTS
  (WJ) SAY AT&T STK MAY FALL -4-
```

SOURCE: By permission of Dow Jones
News/Retrieval.

Text-Search

Supplementing the Dow Jones News database is the Text-Search database. In essence, it is a library of selected news articles that have appeared in *The Wall Street Journal, Barron's,* and the Dow Jones News Service since June 1979. In addition, all news articles that have appeared in *The Wall Street Journal* or the *Washington Post* since January 1984 are available.

You can search for news using any words, phrases, names, dates, or numbers contained in the headlines or text of any of these articles. Specialized search statements can be designed by linking several words together.

EXHIBIT 8–4   Current Stock Quotes for Five Companies

```
//CQE

ENHANCED QUOTES BEING ACCESSED

ENTER QUERY
    AAPL EK GM IBM LOTS

STOCK      BID        ASKED
           CLOSE      OPEN      HIGH        LOW       LAST        VOL(100'S)
AAPL       25 5/8     25 7/8    25 7/8      25 1/4    25 1/2      3937
EK         56 7/8     57        57          55 5/8    55 7/8      19382
GM         79 1/2     80        80 3/8      78 5/8    79 1/4      10048
IBM        155 7/8    156 3/4   156 3/4     152       152 5/8     24884
LOTS       24         24        24 1/2      23 3/4    24          1496

NEWS AVAILABLE FOR EK 10:10am, IBM 11:35am
```

SOURCE: By permission of Dow Jones News/Retrieval.

The Text-Search database is a powerful tool for performing research. It can save you a tremendous amount of time and ensure that you have not missed key news on a company that could affect your investment decisions adversely.

Enhanced Current Quotes

The Enhanced Current Quotes database allows you to obtain prices on common and preferred stocks, NASDAQ over-the-counter stocks, warrants, options, corporate bonds, foreign bonds, mutual funds, U.S. Treasury issues, and government securities. All prices are delayed at least 15 minutes. The database also has a useful news alert feature that automatically advises you when the company you are looking at is making news. Once alerted, you can look for that news through the Dow Jones News database.

Obtaining current quotes is a simple task. Typing a stock symbol and the enter key gives you the previous day's closing price, current day's opening price, and the high, low, and last price quoted along with cumulative trading volume. You can obtain current quotes for up to five securities at a time by pressing the space bar between each symbol (see Exhibit 8–4).

Enhanced Current Quotes is one of the most used databases on DJNR. In addition to direct access, numerous investment software packages, such as Dow Jones Market Manager Plus, automatically access this database to update information on securities included in users' portfolios.

EXHIBIT 8–5 Historical Quotes for IBM

```
//HQ

HISTORICAL QUOTES  BEING ACCESSED

ENTER QUERY
    IBM 85 M


DOW JONES HISTORICAL
STOCK QUOTE REPORTER SERVICE


STOCK   IBM

    1985   MONTHLY SUMMARY
    DATE        HIGH        LOW         CLOSE       VOL.(100/S)
01/85       137 5/8     119         136 3/8     326605
02/85       138 1/4     130 3/4     134         229795
03/85       136 3/4     124 1/8     127         257575
04/85       130 3/8     123 7/8     126 1/2     196036
05/85       133 1/4     124 5/8     128 5/8     249414
06/85       130 5/8     117 3/8     123 3/4     297728
07/85       132 1/2     120         131 3/8     277838
08/85       132 3/4     125 1/2     126 5/8     170279
09/85       130 1/2     122 1/4     123 7/8     231145
10/85       131 3/8     122 7/8     129 7/8     264709
11/85       140 3/4     129 5/8     139 3/4     272732
12/85       158 3/4     137 5/8     155 1/2     286449

* COMPOSITE QUOTES BEGIN WITH OCTOBER 1981
```

SOURCE: By permission of Dow Jones News/Retrieval.

Real-Time Quotes

If you want prices on stocks without the normal 15-minute delay, you can pay an additional monthly charge and access the Real-Time Quotes database. Real-time quotes are available for all stocks trading on the New York, American, Pacific, and Midwest exchanges.

Dow Jones Historical Quotes

For historical stock quotes, you can access the Historical Quotes database. Daily quotes are available for one year, monthly quotes are available from 1979, and quarterly quotes can be retrieved from 1978. A monthly summary for 1985 for IBM is provided in Exhibit 8–5.

Standard & Poor's Online

The Standard & Poor's Online database contains concise profiles of more than 4,600 companies. By entering a stock symbol, you can view a business summary, recent market activity, and dividend information. Product-line summaries and earnings estimates are also provided for most major companies.

Media General Financial Services

The Media General Financial Services database is perhaps one of the most useful databases on DJNR. It provides a concise summary of a company's or industry's price and volume data, as well as fundamental data. Detailed financial information is available for over 4,300 companies and 180 industry groups.

The price and volume data includes stock-price action and volume as shown in Exhibit 8–6. It is obtained by simply entering a stock symbol or industry code, a slash (/), and a P, and then pressing the enter key.

Fundamental data includes revenues, earnings, dividends, ratios, and shareholdings. Entering a stock symbol or industry code, a slash (/), an F, and pressing the enter key will generate a report on fundamental data as illustrated in Exhibit 8–7.

Disclosure II

If you want to view more extensive financial and descriptive data, you can also access the Disclosure II database. It contains a variety of financial reports as shown in Exhibit 8–8. Information can be retrieved by stock symbol for over 10,000 companies. It is extracted from 10-K, 10-Q, 8-K, proxy statements, annual reports to shareholders, tender offers, and registration statements filed with the Securities and Exchange Commission.

Corporate Earnings Estimator

Ultimately, a company's success depends on its profitability. The price of a company's stock not only reflects the current earnings of a company, but also anticipates future earnings. The Corporate

EXHIBIT 8–6 Media General's Price and Volume Data for IBM

//MEDGEN

MEDIA GENERAL–
FINANCIAL SERVICES, INC.
COPYRIGHT (C) 1986
ALL RIGHTS RESERVED

HAVE YOU MADE USE OF MEDIA
GENERAL IN THE LAST MONTH AND
ARE YOU AWARE OF THE NECESSARY
DISCLAIMERS?

ENTER N IF NO,   OR

ENTER QUERY
    IBM/P

INTERNATL BUSINESS MACH
–PRICE & VOLUME– 02/21/86   (170)

PRICE CHANGE   (1)
–LAST TRDNG WK 2.2%
–LAST 4 WKS 6.5%
–LAST 13 WKS 14.5%
–LAST 52 WKS 20.2%
–YR TO DATE 2.7%
CHANGE VS. S & P 500
–LAST TRDNG WK 100%
–LAST 4 WKS 98%
–LAST 13 WKS 103%
–LAST 52 WKS 96%
–YR TO DATE 97%

PRICE RANGE   (2)
–LAST CLOSE $159.75
–52 WEEK HIGH $161.00
–52 WEEK LOW $117.38
–5 YEAR HIGH $161.00
–5 YEAR LOW $48.38
RELATIVE PRICE
–P/E RATIO CURRENT 15.0
–P/E RATIO 5 YR AVG HI 13.3
–P/E RATIO 5 YR AVG LOW 9.2
–PRICE TO COMMON EQUITY 370%
–PRICE TO REV PER SHARE 196%
–RELATIVE PRICE INDEX 127%

PRICE ACTION   (3)
–BETAS UP 1.09
–BETAS DOWN 0.66
VOLUME
–THIS WK SHRS 6,594,000
–THIS WK DOLLAR $1,047,195,000
–THIS WK % SHRS OUTSTND 1.07%
–LIQUIDITY RATIO 47,899,000
–ON BALANCE INDEX 136

SOURCE: By permission of Dow Jones News/Retrieval.

EXHIBIT 8–7 Media General's Fundamental Data for IBM

//MEDGEN

MEDIA GENERAL–
FINANCIAL SERVICES, INC.
COPYRIGHT (C) 1986
ALL RIGHTS RESERVED

HAVE YOU MADE USE OF MEDIA
GENERAL IN THE LAST MONTH AND
ARE YOU AWARE OF THE NECESSARY
DISCLAIMERS?

ENTER N IF NO,   OR

ENTER QUERY
    IBM/F

INTERNATL BUSINESS MACH
–FUNDMNTL DATA– 02/21/86   (170)
REVENUE   (1)
–LAST 12 MOS $50,056 MIL
–LAST FISCAL YEAR $45,937 MIL
–PCT CHANGE LAST QTR 18.3%
–PCT CHANGE YR TO DATE 9.0%
EARNGS 12MOS $6,555.0F MIL
EARNINGS PER SHARE
–LAST 12 MONTHS $10.67
–LAST FISCAL YEAR $10.67
–PCT CHANGE LAST QTR 22.8%
–PCT CHANGE FY TO DATE –0.9%
–PCT CHANGE LAST 12MOS –0.9%
–FIVE YR GROWTH RATE 14.0%

DIVIDENDS   (2)
–CURRENT RATE $4.40
–CURRENT RATE YIELD 2.8%
–5 YR GROWTH RATE 5.0%
–PAYOUT LAST FY 41%
–PAYOUT LAST 5 YEARS 43%
–LAST X–DVD DATE 02–07–86
RATIOS
–PROFIT MARGIN 13.1%
–RETURN ON COMMON EQUITY 24.8%
–RETURN ON TOTAL ASSETS 15.3%
–REVENUE TO ASSETS 117%
–DEBT TO EQUITY 12%
–INTEREST COVERAGE 29.4
–CURRENT RATIO 2.1

SHAREHOLDINGS   (3)
–MARKET VALUE $98,220 MIL
–LTST SHR OUTSTND 614,837,000
–INSIDER NET TRADING –2,000
–SHORT INTEREST RATIO 2.0 DYS
–FISCAL YEAR ENDS 12 MOS

SOURCE: By permission of Dow Jones News/Retrieval.

EXHIBIT 8–8   Disclosure II Reports Available for IBM

```
//DSCLO

DISCLOSURE II
COPYRIGHT (C) 1986
DISCLOSURE INC.

FINANCIAL AND MANAGEMENT
INFORMATION ON PUBLIC
CORPORATIONS BASED ON REPORTS
FILED WITH THE SECURITIES AND
EXCHANGE COMMISSION (NOTE: THERE IS A
$6 PRIME-TIME ACCESS CHARGE FOR EACH
COMPANY REPORT; $2 IN NON-PRIME TIME.)


------------------------------------
TO CONTINUE, ENTER COMPANY STOCK
SYMBOL AND PRESS RETURN
    IBM

COMPANY NAME:          INTERNATIONAL BUSINESS MACHINES CORP

ENTER    FOR

   1     CORPORATE PROFILE
   2     BALANCE SHEETS FOR 2 YEARS
   3     INCOME STATEMENTS FOR 3 YEARS
   4     QTRLY INC STATEMENTS (CUR FY)
   5     LINE OF BUSINESS DATA
   6     5-YR SUMMARY DATA (REVS, INCOME,
            EPS)
   7     FULL FINANCIAL DATA (2 THRU 6)
   8     OFFICERS AND DIRECTORS
   9     OWNERSHIP AND SUBSIDIARIES
  10     OTHER CORPORATE EVENTS
  11     MANAGEMENT DISCUSSION
  12     CORPORATE RECORD (1 THRU 10)
  13     FULL CORPORATE RECORD (1 THRU 11)
  14     2-YR LIST OF REPORTS ON FILE
            WITH THE SEC
  99     HOW TO ORDER FULL TEXT OF SEC
            REPORTS
```

SOURCE: By permission of Dow Jones News/Retrieval.

Earnings Estimator database gives you a way to examine professionals' forecasts.

The Corporate Earnings Estimator database provides forecasts of earnings per share for 3,000 widely followed companies based on estimates provided by 1,000 top Wall Street analysts at more than 60 major brokerage firms. For each company, the database shows the average of the latest earnings per share estimates, as well as high and low estimates for each of the next two fiscal years. In addition, estimates dating back 4, 13, and 26 weeks are shown so you can compare analysts' current estimates to prior

---

EXHIBIT 8–9 Earnings Forecast
for IBM

```
//EARN

CORPORATE EARNINGS ESTIMATOR
PLEASE ENTER DESIRED STOCK
SYMBOL AND PRESS RETURN    IBM

IBM
--FISCAL YEAR ENDS  12/86

EARNINGS PER SHARE ESTIMATES
--MEAN    12.69
--HIGH    13.50
--LOW     11.75
NUMBER OF ANALYSTS   33
P/E RATIO (ESTIMATED EPS)   11.90

PAST EARN PR SH ESTIMATES (MEAN)
--WEEK AGO     12.69
--13 WEEKS AGO   12.80
--26 WEEKS AGO   12.91

-----------------------------------
PRESS RETURN FOR NEXT PAGE

IBM
--FISCAL YEAR ENDS  12/87

EARNINGS PER SHARE ESTIMATES
--MEAN    14.97
--HIGH    15.50
--LOW     14.40
NUMBER OF ANALYSTS    4
P/E RATIO (ESTIMATED EPS)   10.09

PAST EARN PR SH ESTIMATES (MEAN)
--WEEK AGO     14.97
--13 WEEKS AGO   14.50
--26 WEEKS AGO    N/A
Press <CR> for more !
```

SOURCE: By permission of Dow
Jones News/Retrieval.

projections. The database is updated weekly. A sample earnings forecast for IBM is shown in Exhibit 8–9.

Investext

Leading stock brokerage firms constantly release research reports on individual companies. Unless you are a major client of one of the brokerage firms, these reports normally are not available to you. However, through the Investext database, you can now access thousands of these reports containing current, forecasted, and historical marketing and financial information.

EXHIBIT 8–10   Ticker Retrieval Reports Menu for IBM

```
CompuServe                    TICKER



Enter a ticker (ie, HRB), a CUSIP number (ie, 09367110),
or an asterisk followed by the beginning of a company's
name (ie, *BLOCK).  Type /M to exit or /HELP for cost
information and instructions.

Company: IBM




INTERNATIONAL BUSINESS MACHINE(IBM)    CUSIP number:    45920010
                                        Exchange:       N

  Date     Time    Volume      High    Low      Last     Change
 ------   ------  --------    ------  -----    ------    --------
 2/07/86  16:13   1,832,700   157 1/4  151     155 3/4   +1 7/8

 1 Descriptive company info      9 Annual financial statements
 2 Price history from 12/31/73  10 Quarterly rpt as of 9/30/85
 3 Dividends from 2/05/68       11 I/B/E/S & Value Line Forecast
 4 Price stats, last 52 weeks   12 Officers, directors, salaries
 5 Detailed issue description
 6 Bonds issued, appx 5         14 Full Disclosure II info
 7 Options issued, appx 84
 8 Return on $1000 invested

Enter choice !
```

SOURCE: By permission of CompuServe, Inc.

COMPUSERVE

Another on-line service for investors is CompuServe. Compu-
Serve, like DJNR, enables you to retrieve current and historical
prices for securities, descriptive company information, financial
statements, and earnings estimates. Of particular value to investors seeking specific company information is CompuServe's Ticker
Retrieval feature.

With Ticker Retrieval, you enter a ticker symbol or a CUSIP
number for a security, and the service provides the current market
price quotation and a menu that lists additional information available on that company. For example, if you enter IBM, you receive
the current price for International Business Machines followed
by the menu illustrated in Exhibit 8–10 that lists the descriptive

EXHIBIT 8–11 Monthly Price History for IBM

```
(D)aily, (W)eekly, (M)onthly? : M

Starting date or <CR> for number of
periods from last pricing date? 2/1/85
Ending date    :    2/1/86




                   INTERNATIONAL BUSINESS MACHS

Cusip: 45920010          Exchange: N          Ticker: IBM

Month-End      Months          Months          Months        Month-End
   Date        Volume         High/Ask         Low/Bid        Close/Avg
----------    -----------    -----------     -----------     -----------
  2/28/85     22,979,700     138 1/4         130 3/4         134
  3/29/85     25,682,800     136 3/4         124 1/8         127

  4/30/85     19,606,300     130 3/8         123 7/8         126 1/2
  5/31/85     24,937,900     133 1/4         124 5/8         128 5/8
  6/28/85     29,774,000     130 5/8         117 3/8         123 3/4

  7/31/85     27,787,500     132 1/2         120             131 3/8
  8/30/85     17,032,100     132 3/4         125 1/2         126 5/8
  9/30/85     23,115,700     130 1/2         122 1/4         123 7/8

 10/31/85     26,470,400     131 3/8         122 7/8         129 7/8

Press <CR> for more !




Month-End      Months          Months          Months        Month-End
   Date        Volume         High/Ask         Low/Bid        Close/Avg
----------    -----------    -----------     -----------     -----------
 11/29/85     27,275,000     140 3/4         129 5/8         139 3/4
 12/31/85     28,617,300     158 3/4         137 5/8         155 1/2

  1/31/86     31,895,000     156 1/2         143             151 1/2
  2/06/86*     5,500,600     156             151 5/8         155

          * indicates a partial period

Prices Available: 12/31/73 through 2/06/86

Last page !
```

SOURCE: By permission of CompuServe, Inc.

EXHIBIT 8–12   Dividend Summary for IBM

```
Starting date or <CR> for number of
periods from last pricing date? 1/1/83
Ending date   :    12/31/85




                INTERNATIONAL BUSINESS MACHS

Cusip: 45920010      Exchange: N     Ticker: IBM

   Rate          Type        Ex-Date         Record        Payment
-------------------------------------------------------------------
$  0.860        Cash        2/03/83        2/09/83        3/10/83
$  0.950        Cash        5/05/83        5/11/83        6/10/83
$  0.950        Cash        8/04/83        8/10/83        9/10/83
$  0.950        Cash        11/02/83       11/09/83       12/10/83
$  0.950        Cash        2/03/84        2/09/84        3/10/84
$  0.950        Cash        5/04/84        5/10/84        6/09/84
$  1.100        Cash        8/08/84        8/14/84        9/10/84
$  1.100        Cash        10/31/84       11/07/84       12/10/84
$  1.100        Cash        2/06/85        2/13/85        3/09/85
$  1.100        Cash        5/03/85        5/09/85        6/10/85
$  1.100        Cash        8/08/85        8/14/85        9/10/85
$  1.100        Cash        11/06/85       11/13/85       12/10/85

Last page !
```

SOURCE: By permission of CompuServe, Inc.

and financial information available for IBM. This menu leads you to all of the information you need to make an investment decision.

Monthly Price History

Selecting choice 2 from the Ticker Retrieval menu enables you to obtain daily, weekly, and monthly price quotes for a company going back 12 years. Exhibit 8–11 shows a summary of the monthly volume, high, low, and closing prices for IBM for a 12-month period.

Dividend Summary

Choice 3 from the Ticker Retrieval menu allows you to examine a summary of dividends paid from 1968 to date or for any period in between. To illustrate, a dividend summary for a three-year period for IBM is shown in Exhibit 8–12.

EXHIBIT 8–13   Value Line's Financial
Statements for IBM

```
            INT'L BUSINESS MACH
            Income Statement
                         12/83      12/84
                       ----------  ----------
Gross Revenues          40180.00   45937.00
  Cost of Goods Sold    12457.00   15704.00
  Selling & Admin Exp   14196.00   15787.00
  Depreciation, Amort    3938.00    3215.00
  Total Interest          390.00     408.00
  Unconsolidated Subs       0.00       0.00
  Other Income            741.00     800.00
  Other Expenses           0.00       0.00
  Minority Interest        0.00       0.00
                       ----------  ----------
Pretax Income            9940.00   11623.00

  Total Taxes            4455.00    5041.00
  Special Items             0.00       0.00
                       ----------  ----------
Net Income Before Ext    5485.00    6582.00
  Extraordinary Items       0.00       0.00

Press <CR> for more !


            INT'L BUSINESS MACH
            Balance Sheet
                         12/83      12/84
                       ----------  ----------
Cash & Equivalents       5536.00    4362.00
Accounts Receivable      6380.00    8111.00
Inventories              4381.00    6598.00
Other Current Assets      973.00    1304.00
                       ----------  ----------
Total Current Assets    17270.00   20375.00

Gross Plant             29187.00   29423.00
  Accum Depreciation    13045.00   13060.00
Net Plant               16142.00   16363.00
Long-Term Investments    3831.00    4784.00
Deferred Charges            0.00       0.00
Intangible Assets           0.00    1286.00
Other Long-Term Asset       0.00       0.00
                       ----------  ----------
Total Assets            37243.00   42808.00

Press <CR> for more !
```

Obtaining Financial Reports

Choice 9 from the Ticker Retrieval menu provides another menu
that gives you a choice of financial statements from Value Line or
Disclosure II. Exhibit 8–13 shows the annual financial statements
available from Value Line, which presents two years of information
in a comparative format. Value Line gives an income statement,

EXHIBIT 8–13 *(continued)*

```
Balance Sheet (cont.)
                           12/83       12/84
                        ----------  ----------

Notes Payable              284.00      361.00
Accounts Payable          1253.00     1618.00
Taxes Payable             3220.00     2668.00
Other Current Liab        4502.00     4520.00
Deferred Taxes             713.00     2057.00
Minority Interest            0.00        0.00
Long-Term Debt            2922.00     3742.00
Other Long-Term Liab      1130.00     1353.00
                        ----------  ----------

Total Liabilities        14024.00    16319.00

Preferred Stock              N/A         N/A
Common Stock              5800.00     5998.00
Additional Capital           N/A         N/A
Retained Earnings        19489.00    23439.00
                        ----------  ----------

Press <CR> for more !

Total Equity             25289.00    29437.00


            INT'L BUSINESS MACH
              Sources & Uses
                           12/83       12/84
                        ----------  ----------

Cash Flow                 9423.00     9797.00
Property Sales            2108.00     1483.00
Common Financing           788.00       73.00
Preferred Financing          0.00        0.00
Long-Term Debt Financ      174.00     1363.00
Other Sources              175.00     1571.00

Capital Spending          4930.00     5473.00
Other Investments         2178.00     2567.00
Common Retired               0.00        0.00
Preferred Retired            0.00        0.00
Debt Retired               351.00      768.00
Common Dividends          2251.00     2507.00
Preferred Dividends          0.00        0.00
Add'l Working Capital     2958.00     2972.00

Press <CR> for more !
```

balance sheet, sources and uses of funds, and key ratios. The key ratios section of the financial statements can be particularly informative. Disclosure II presents a five-year summary of sales, net income, and primary earnings per share (see Exhibit 8–14).

Ticker Retrieval also provides access to quarterly financial statements for up-to-date information on key financial statement items between releases of annual statements. Choice 10 from the Ticker Retrieval menu provides a quarterly report like the one shown for IBM in Exhibit 8–15.

EXHIBIT 8–13 (concluded)

```
            INT'L BUSINESS MACH
               Key Ratios
                          12/83      12/84
                        ----------  ----------
Earnings Per Share         9.04      10.77
Price/Earnings Ratio      12.72      10.75
Return on Equity          21.69      22.36
Return on Assets          14.73      15.38
Dividends Per Share        3.71       4.10
Dividend Yield             3.22       3.54

Sales / Assets             1.08       1.07
Market/Book Value          3.02       2.67
Current Ratio              1.82       2.11
Quick Ratio                1.36       1.43
Times Interest Earned     26.49      29.49
Beta                       N/A        1.00
Common Shares            610.72     612.69
Net Avail for Common    5485.00    6582.00
```

SOURCE: By permission of CompuServe, Inc.

EXHIBIT 8–14   Disclosure II's Five-Year Summary for IBM

```
            INTERNATIONAL BUSINESS MACHINE
                   5-Year Summary
                12/80      12/81      12/82      12/83      12/84
             ---------- ---------- ---------- ---------- ----------
Sales        26213.00   29070.00   34364.00   40180.00   45937.00
Net Income    3397.00    3610.00    4409.00    5485.00    6582.00
Net / Sales %   12.96      12.42      12.83      13.65      14.33

Primary EPS      5.82       6.14       7.39       9.04      10.77

Press <CR> for more !
```

SOURCE: By permission of CompuServe, Inc.

Value Line's Three to Five Year Forecasts

You can also examine Value Line's Three to Five Year Forecasts, as illustrated for IBM in Exhibit 8–16. Forecasts are provided for sales, earnings per share, dividends, book value per share, and market price.

PUTTING IT ALL TOGETHER

With Schwab's Investor Information Service, DJNR, and CompuServe, you have a vast amount of company information available at your fingertips. Using these on-line services to obtain

EXHIBIT 8–15   Value Line's Quarterly Financial Statements for IBM

```
                            INT'L BUSINESS MACH
                   VALUE LINE QUARTERLY FINANCIALS

                        Fiscal Quarters
                   ---------------------------
                       3/85        6/85        9/85        12/85
                      ------      ------      ------      -------

Sales or Revenues     9769.00    11434.00    11698.00    17155.00
Earnings Per Share*      1.610       2.300       2.400       4.360
Net Income             986.00     1414.00     1474.00     2681.00

                       Calendar Quarters
                   ---------------------------
                       3/85        6/85        9/85        12/85
                      ------      ------      ------      -------

Dividends Per Share      1.100       1.100       1.100       1.100
Average Weekly Price   129.923     126.692     127.355     138.392
Ending Weekly Price    127.000     123.750     123.875     155.500
High Price             138.250     133.250     132.750     158.750
Low Price              119.000     117.375     120.000     122.875
```

*Earnings per share type: Primary

Last page !

SOURCE: By permission of CompuServe, Inc.

EXHIBIT 8–16   Value Line's Three-to Five-Year Forecasts for IBM

```
              INT'L BUSINESS MACH
              Value Line Forecasts
              3 - 5 Year Projection

Forecast period falls between  1988-1990

Shares Outstanding              623.00
Sales                         83014.75
Earnings Per Share               19.00
Dividends Per Share               7.60
Book Value Per Share             82.00
High Target Price               270.00
Low Target Price                220.00
% Appreciation High              80.00
% Appreciation Low               45.00

Estimated EPS For 12-Month Per
Ending 6 Months Hence            12.01
Estimated Dividends Per Share
Next 12 Months                    4.40
```

Last page !

SOURCE: By permission of CompuServe, Inc.

the latest news, financial statements, earnings estimates, and other key information enables you to have all the facts you need to make a truly informed investment decision.

APPENDIX: TIPS ON SAVING CONNECT CHARGES

On-line services, such as DJNR and CompuServe, typically charge by the minute or by the hour for the actual time you are connected to the on-line service. Therefore, minimizing the correct time is important.

There are several ways to control on-line costs. First, always plan your on-line sessions thoroughly before you sign on. With the massive amounts of financial information at your fingertips, you may be tempted to sign on and go from one feature to another, looking at information that is interesting but of little practical value in managing your investments. This is the quickest way to build up high charges. Avoid it by taking a few minutes to map out the features you will access and the specific information you will retrieve first. Then sign on, retrieve the required information in an orderly and efficient manner, and sign off.

Often, you will want to print the information being reviewed on-line for further study after you sign off. Most printers are relatively slow compared to the speed with which you can save information on a disk. Therefore, save the information on a disk and print it after you sign off—when you are not paying for connect time.

Whenever possible, access the on-line services during non-business hours (evenings and weekends). By doing so you can retrieve the same information at savings of up to 80 percent of the rate charged during peak business hours.

Finally, retrieve data at the highest transmission speed possible. Although charges for 1200-baud transmission are normally twice that for 300-baud transmission, you receive information four times as fast resulting in a lower overall cost.

PART 4

Technical Analysis

CHAPTER 9

Taking a Picture of Stock Market Activity

Technicians, as those who perform technical analysis are called, do not believe that the price of stocks and the overall stock market moves in a random manner. Rather, they contend that there is a direct relationship between price movements in the past and those that will occur in the future. Their objective is to determine what this relationship is so that they will be able to accurately predict whether the stock market or a particular stock will go up or down.

The primary tool that a technician uses for analysis is a picture or chart of a stock's price movement. Bar charts are by far the most common type of price charts used. In a bar chart, each period is represented by a vertical line that ranges from the period's low to its high. The period's closing price is indicated by a horizontal protrusion.

The length of the period varies depending on whether you want short-term, intermediate-term, or long-term information. There is no generally accepted definition of short-term, intermediate-term, and long-term. But short-term is normally associated with the next three months, intermediate-term can be thought of as three to six months from the present, and long-term can be defined as the period of six months to one year from the current period.

Hourly and daily bar charts are often used to determine the short-term trend of stock price movements. Weekly charts are used to gain an intermediate-term perspective. Monthly and yearly charts are helpful in examining the long term.

ANALYZING INDIVIDUAL SECURITIES

By looking at a bar chart, the technician attempts to discover at a glance some discernable trend in the stock's price movement.

EXHIBIT 9–1 Twelve-Year Bar Chart for IBM

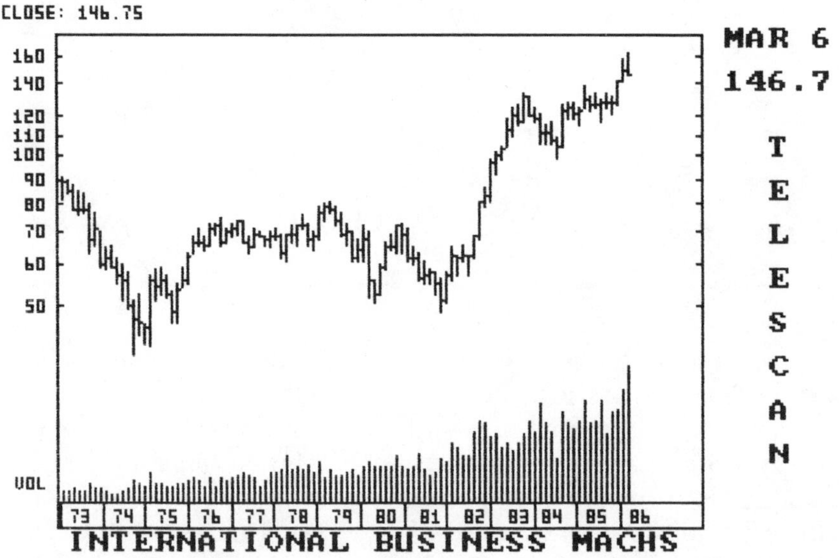
CLOSE: 146.75
MAR 6
146.7
160
140
120
110
100
90
80
70
60
50
VOL
73 74 75 76 77 78 79 80 81 82 83 84 85 86
INTERNATIONAL BUSINESS MACHS
T E L E S C A N

SOURCE: By permission of Telescan, Inc.

Let's look at two sample bar charts—one long-term and one short-term.

Exhibit 9–1 shows 12 years of price and volume activity for IBM. At the beginning of the period, 1973 to mid-1974, the stock was clearly in a downtrend. After a short upturn during 1975, the stock's price trend was basically sideways until the end of 1981. Since that time IBM has been in a strong uptrend with a little sideways movement during 1983 and 1984. Based on this chart, you would conclude that the long-term trend for IBM is up.

Let's look at a short-term chart for IBM. Exhibit 9–2 shows a daily bar chart for a six-month period. Between September and the middle of October, IBM basically moved sideways, with no clear direction up or down. However, between the middle of October and end of February, the price of IBM's stock shot up from about \$125 per share to over \$155 per share. During the end of February and the beginning of March, the stock's price has moved down slightly. However, by glancing at this chart, you would conclude that the short-term trend is up.

Notice the volume histogram at the bottom of both Exhibits 9–1 and 9–2. It is common for volume to be shown in this manner

EXHIBIT 9–2   Six-Month Bar Chart for IBM with a 20-Day Moving
Average Line

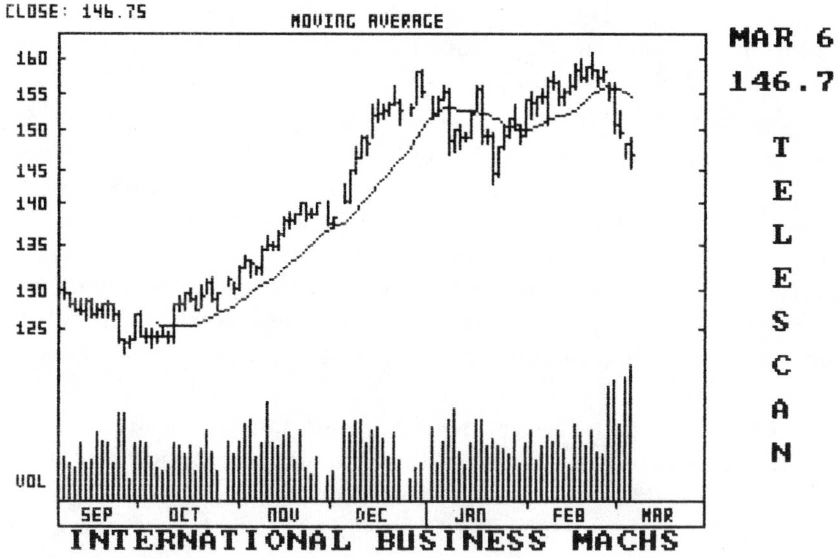

CLOSE: 146.75

MOVING AVERAGE

MAR 6
146.7

T
E
L
E
S
C
A
N

INTERNATIONAL BUSINESS MACHS

SOURCE: By permission of Telescan, Inc.

at the bottom of a bar chart. Normally, strength is indicated by rising volume when a stock's price is going up or shrinking volume when price is declining. Weakness is shown by rising volume on a decline in price and declining volume on an advance in price. Volume is often monitored as a leading indicator since volume trends tend to reverse before price trends.

In addition to volume, other technical indicators are often plotted, such as moving averages, oscillators, momentum (rate of change), and relative strength.

Moving averages are frequently used to smooth price fluctuations. They enable the technician to get a clearer picture of the trend of the stock being studied. A moving average is just what the name implies, an average that moves with the period of time covered. For example, a 10-day moving average is calculated by adding up the stock's closing price for each of the last 10 days and dividing by 10. Each day you add the latest day's price, subtract the price for 10 days ago, and divide the new total by 10.

Technicians use different time frames for moving averages depending on their perspectives. Often 50-day, 100-day, and 200-

day moving averages are used for short-term, intermediate-term, and long-term analysis, respectively.

As a rule of thumb, as long as a stock's price is above its moving average line, the outlook is bullish. On the other hand, if it is below its moving average line, it is a bearish or negative sign. Exhibit 9–2 shows a 20-day moving average line for IBM.

Another indicator that is frequently used is relative strength. Relative strength compares the performance of a stock to another stock, an industry group, or an overall market index, such as the Dow Jones Industrial Average. If you compare the relative strength of a particular stock with the Dow Jones Industrial Average, the resulting chart will show whether or not the stock is moving up or down at the same pace as the overall stock market. Ideally, you want to locate stocks that outperform, that is move up relatively faster than, the overall market.

A wide range of other sophisticated indicators are used to analyze individual securities. These include commodity channel index, commodity selection index, demand index, detrend, directional movement index, HAL momentum index, momentum, on balance volume, oscillator, parabolic, rate of change, relative strength index, stochastic, volume accumulation, Williams % R, and many others. Each indicator is calculated using only three basic items: price, volume, and, in the case of some commodities and futures, open interest.

TECHNICAL MARKET INDICATORS

In addition to the indicators used to analyze individual securities, a large body of technical market indicators is used to evaluate the overall stock market. The technician tracks these indicators because of the importance of the movement of the overall stock market.

Most stocks move in the same direction as the overall stock market. If the overall stock market is moving up, the majority of stocks will move up; if the overall stock market is moving down, the majority of stocks will also move down. Since most stocks move with the overall market, most Wall Street analysts feel that determining the trend of the overall stock market is essential to successful investing.

Technical market indicators used to determine the trend of the overall market are normally divided into three types: momentum, sentiment, and monetary. Momentum indicators are designed to show market strength and weakness and include rate of change, advance/decline, volume, and new high/low indicators.

Sentiment indicators examine investor expectations and their opinions regarding the stock market. Many sentiment indicators are based on the concept that investors are usually wrong about the direction of the stock market and, therefore, these indicators are normally used as contrary indicators. That is, if a sentiment indicator shows that investors are enthusiastic about the future of the stock market and believe it is going to go up, it is likely that the stock market will go down. Popular sentiment indicators include short sales, odd-lot trades, and the put/call ratio.

Monetary indicators revolve around the concept that when interest rates go down the stock market goes up and when interest rates go up the stock market goes down. The logic is that investors want to have their money in the investment vehicle that is likely to yield the greatest return. If interest rates decline, the yield you receive on investments such as money market funds and certificates of deposit also declines. Therefore, interest-based investments become less attractive and stocks become more attractive since investors are more likely to get a better return in the stock market.

Let's look at a specific indicator—the advance/decline line. The advance/decline line is a momentum indicator. It is the most common measure of market breadth and is considered to be one of the most important technical indicators of the stock market.

Market breadth refers to the number of stocks that are advancing or declining. When the majority of stocks are moving up at the same time as the overall stock market is advancing, the market is said to have good breadth.

The advance/decline line is calculated by taking the difference between the number of stocks that advanced in price for the day and the number of stocks that declined in price for the day. This figure is then added or subtracted to a cumulative number every day in order to determine the advance/decline line.

In general, the purpose of the advance/decline line is to provide a warning of whether the market as a whole is gaining or losing strength. Specifically, it is used to identify a major change in the direction of the market before any of the market indices do. For example, when the Dow Jones Industrial Average is going up and the advance/decline line is going down, it is a signal that

EXHIBIT 9-3 Advance/Decline Line (top half) and Standard & Poor's 500 Index (bottom half)

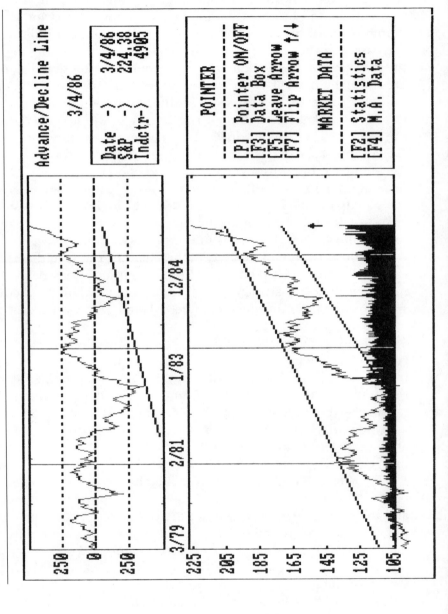

EXHIBIT 9–4   Six-Month Bar Chart for IBM with Trendline

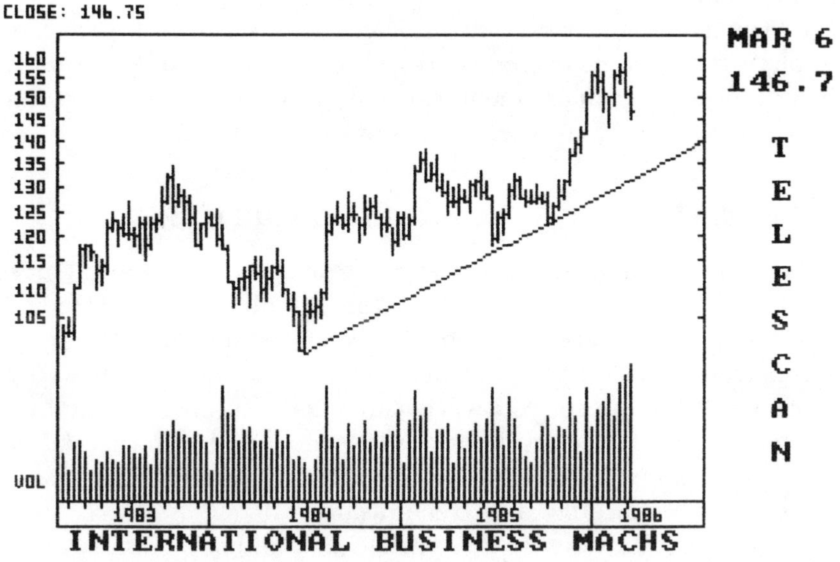

SOURCE: By permission of Telescan, Inc.

the technical condition of the market is deteriorating and the market may turn down soon.

Exhibit 9–3 shows the advance/decline line for a five-year period. On the bottom half of the screen a broad stock market index, the Standard & Poor's 500 Index, is shown.

Other technical market indicators serve the same function as the advance/decline line to provide a warning of the overall direction of the stock market.

CHART ANALYSIS TOOLS

Technicians use a variety of chart analysis tools in conjunction with bar charts and indicator charts. These include trendlines, parallel trendlines, support and resistance lines, 1/3—2/3 speed resistance lines, trading bands (also known as envelopes), and cycles.

Of these charting tools, the trendline is the most widely used. A trendline connects a series of stock prices, tops or bottoms, by a straight line as illustrated in Exhibit 9–4. These lines are simple but important chart analysis tools since they are reliable about 80 percent of the time in predicting reversals in stock trends. A reversal in a stock trend is indicated when the trendline is penetrated significantly.

Preparing bar charts and indicator charts and utilizing chart analysis tools can be extremely time-consuming if done manually. Fortunately, you can use technical analysis software and a personal computer to speed up the process dramatically.

SELECTING TECHNICAL ANALYSIS SOFTWARE

When selecting a technical analysis software package that will meet your specific needs, numerous factors should be considered. A good way to compare alternative packages is to complete a questionnaire similar to the one provided in Exhibit 9–5 for each package. By doing so, you will ensure that you have entertained all of the important considerations in evaluating technical analysis software. Exhibit 9–6 shows a completed technical analysis software questionnaire for The Technician.

Technical analysis software packages should be examined from a variety of angles. First, determine the type of data required to use the package and the sources for such data. Technical analysis software packages require the input of extensive information in order to prepare charts. For example, if you want to see a basic high-low-close-volume bar chart for IBM for a 90-day period, the program will require 450 items of data. Although you can manually enter this data into the computer via the keyboard, most programs have the ability to obtain the required data from an on-line service, such as the Dow Jones News/Retrieval. This method of retrieval will greatly reduce the time needed to create a chart and, if you wish, enable you to expand the number of stocks you follow.

In examining the charting features for each package, look for a variety of features of value to the technician. First, determine whether charts can be displayed in color on the screen. Although this is not an essential feature, it can be helpful when more than one security or technical indicator is plotted on the same chart. For example, assume you plot both a 10-day and a 50-day moving average line on a bar chart for a particular stock. To distinguish the 10-day moving average line from the 50-day moving average line, it is helpful to have each appear in a different color.

EXHIBIT 9–5 Technical Analysis Software Questionnaire—IBM PC Systems

GENERAL INFORMATION

Product name: _____   Version #: _____
Vendor name: _____
Address: _____
_____
_____

Telephone: _____
List price: _____
Demonstration diskette available? _____ Yes _____ No
    If yes, what is the price of the demonstration diskette? _____
Money-back guarantee available? _____ Yes _____ No
    If yes, how many days? _____

HARDWARE REQUIREMENTS

Operating system: _____ DOS 1.1 or later _____Other (Specify) _____
_____ DOS 2.0 or later
Minimum memory required: _____ 64K _____ 128K _____ 192K _____ 256K
Number of disk drives required: _____ 1 single-sided
_____ 2 single-sided
_____ 1 double-sided
_____ 2 double-sided
Other _____
Color graphics required? _____ Yes _____ No
Modem required? _____ Yes _____ No
Modem recommended? _____ Yes _____ No
Printer required? _____ Yes _____ No
Printer recommended? _____ Yes _____ No
Other hardware requirements (specify): _____
_____
_____
_____

PRODUCT SUPPORT

Who provides support for the product? _____
Is there a telephone number available for support? _____ Yes _____ No
    If yes, is it toll-free? _____ Yes _____ No
    Days of the week support is available: _____
    Hours of the day support is available: _____
Is the software copy protected? _____ Yes _____ No
    If yes, can you copy program to a hard disk? _____ Yes _____ No
    Cost of backup copy? _____
Defective disk replacement policy: _____
_____
_____

Update policy: _____
_____
_____

EXHIBIT 9–5 *(continued)*

DOCUMENTATION

Number of pages in user's manual? _____

User's manual includes:	Yes	No
Tutorial	____	____
Index	____	____
Glossary	____	____
Explanation of error messages	____	____
Sample applications	____	____
Samples of screen displays	____	____
Samples of printed output	____	____

Does the package include a tutorial on disk? _____ Yes _____ No
Does the package include a reference card? _____ Yes _____ No
Does the disk contain sample applications? _____ Yes _____ No
   If yes, how many and what type? _____
Does the package include a demonstration disk? _____ Yes _____ No

EASE OF USE

Estimated time to learn basic functions:
   ____ Less than 1 day ____ 1 to 6 days ____ 1 to 2 weeks
   ____ over 2 weeks
Commands are abbreviated for quick entry? _____ Yes _____ No
Error messages are provided on screen? _____ Yes _____ No
Programs are menu driven? _____ Yes _____ No
Help screens are available? _____ At all times
                                    _____ At various points in the program
                                      _____ Nonexistent
How experienced with the IBM PC should a person be to use this package?
   ____ Very ____ Somewhat ____ Little ____ No experience

DATA ENTRY

Data is entered? _____ Manually _____ Via modem
                    _____ User's choice of manually or via modem
If data is entered via modem, which on-line database is accessed? (Check all
   that apply)
   _____ Dow Jones News/Retrieval
   _____ CompuServe
   _____ Warner Computer Systems
   _____ Remote Computing
   _____ Other (Specify)_____
   _____ Other (Specify) _____
If data is entered via modem, what type of information is obtained? (Check all
   that apply)
   _____ Current quotes (same day)
   _____ Historical quotes (over one day old)
   _____ Miscellaneous data used to calculate technical market indicators
   _____ Other (Specify) _____
If data is entered via modem, is dialing, log on, retrieval of required data, and
   log off automatic? _____ Yes _____ No

EXHIBIT 9-5 (*continued*)

If data is entered manually, what type of information is entered? (Check all that apply)

_____ Current quotes (same day)

_____ Historical quotes (over one day old)

_____ Miscellaneous data used to calculate technical market indicators

_____ Other (Specify) _____

After data is entered, can it be easily checked and changed?

_____ Yes   _____ No

CHARTING FEATURES

Software produces graphs on the screen in: _____ Color _____ Monochrome

_____ Both

Graphs can be based on which data: (Check all that apply)

_____ Daily   _____ Quarterly

_____ Weekly   _____ Yearly

_____ Monthly

Maximum number of data points that can be plotted on a graph? _____

Are time periods for graphs user definable?   _____ Yes   _____ No

Which of the following types of scaling are permitted? (Check all that apply)

_____ Linear scaling

_____ Logarithmic scaling

_____ Semilogarithmic scaling

Is scaling automatic?   _____ Yes   _____ No

Are scale ranges user definable?   _____ Yes   _____ No

Can you have multiple scales?   _____ Yes   _____ No

Can horizontal grid lines be drawn?   _____ Yes   _____ No

Can vertical grid lines be drawn?   _____ Yes   _____ No

Can customized formulas be entered for calculations and plots?

_____ Yes   _____ No

Can multiple graphs be shown on an individual screen?   _____ Yes _____ No

If yes, how many? _____

Can graphs be saved on a disk?   _____ Yes   _____ No

Can data used in graphs be printed in tables?   _____ Yes   _____ No

Can the user "zoom in" to examine less data on the screen and "zoom out" to examine more data on the screen?   _____ Yes   _____ No

Which of the following items can be plotted?

	Yes	No
High-low-close bar charts	_____	_____
Volume histograms	_____	_____
Moving averages:		
Simple	_____	_____
Weighted	_____	_____
Exponential	_____	_____
Trend lines	_____	_____
Trading bands	_____	_____
Oscillators	_____	_____
Support and resistance lines	_____	_____
Relative strength	_____	_____

EXHIBIT 9–5   (*concluded*)

Cycles   _____   _____
Point & figure charts   _____   _____
Other (Specify) _____

_____

_____

_____

TECHNICAL MARKET INDICATORS
List the technical market indicators that can be produced:

_____

_____

_____

_____

_____

_____

OTHER FEATURES
Does the software have an autorun feature?   _____ Yes   _____ No
Can you produce hard copy of all graphs?   _____ Yes   _____ No
Does the software facilitate testing of trading strategies?   _____ Yes   _____ No

---

EXHIBIT 9–6   Completed Technical Analysis Software Questionnaire for The
Technician—IBM PC Version

GENERAL INFORMATION
Product name: The Technician   Version #: 3.0
Vendor name: Computer Asset Management
Address: P.O. Box 26743
              Salt Lake City, UT 84126

Telephone: (801) 964-0391
List price: $395
Demonstration diskette available?   _X_ Yes   _____ No
    If yes, what is the price of the demonstration diskette? _____ $5
Money-back guarantee available?   _____ Yes   _X_ No
    If yes, how many days? __N/A*__

HARDWARE REQUIREMENTS
Operating system: _____ DOS 1.1 or later   _____ Other (Specify) _____
                  _X_ DOS 2.0 or later
Minimum memory required: _____ 64K _____ 128K _X_ 192K _____ 256K

EXHIBIT 9–6 (*continued*)

Number of disk drives required: _____ 1 single-sided
_____ 2 single-sided
_____ 1 double-sided
_X_ 2 double-sided
Other _____

Color graphics required?	_X_ Yes	_____ No		
Modem required?	_____ Yes	_X_ No		
Modem recommended?	_X_ Yes	_____ No		
Printer required?	_____ Yes	_X_ No		
Printer recommended?	_X_ Yes	_____ No		

Other hardware requirements (specify): None _____

_____
_____
_____

PRODUCT SUPPORT

Who provides support for the product? Computer Asset Management _____
Is there a telephone number available for support? _X_ Yes _____ No
  If yes, is it toll-free? _____ Yes _X_ No
  Days of the week support is available: Monday to Friday _____
  Hours of the day support is available: Business hours _____
Is the software copy protected? _____ Yes _X_ No
  If yes, can you copy program to a hard disk? N/A _____ Yes _____ No
  Cost of backup copy? N/A _____
Defective disk replacement policy: Defective disks are replaced without charge
for one year from date of purchase. _____

_____

Update policy: Updates are provided every 6 to 12 months. The charge for the
last update was $50. _____

_____

DOCUMENTATION

Number of pages in user's manual? _____237_____
User's manual includes:

	Yes	No	
Tutorial	_____	_X_	
Index	_X_	_____	
Glossary	_____	_X_	Note: A 110
Explanation of error messages	_X_	_____	page section
Sample applications	_X_	_____	discusses indicator
Samples of screen displays	_X_	_____	interpretation.
Samples of printed output	_X_	_____	

Does the package include a tutorial on disk? _____ Yes _X_ No
Does the package include a reference card? _X_ Yes _____ No

EXHIBIT 9–6 (*continued*)

Does the disk contain sample applications?   __X__ Yes   _____ No
   If yes, how many and what type? Includes data for seven years
Does the package include a demonstration disk?   _____ Yes __X__ No

EASE OF USE
Estimated time to learn basic functions:
   __X__ Less than 1 day _____ 1 to 6 days _____ 1 to 2 weeks
   _____ over 2 weeks
Commands are abbreviated for quick entry?   __X__ Yes   _____ No
Error messages are provided on screen?   __X__ Yes   _____ No
Programs are menu driven?   __X__ Yes   _____ No
Help screens are available? __X__ At all times
                             _____ At various points in the program
                             _____ Nonexistent
How experienced with the IBM PC should a person be to use this package?
   _____ Very _____ Somewhat __X__ Little _____ No experience

DATA ENTRY
Data is entered?   _____ Manually   _____ Via modem
                  __X__ User's choice of manually or via modem
If data is entered via modem, which on-line database is accessed? (Check all
   that apply)
   _____ Dow Jones News/Retrieval
   _____ CompuServe
   _____ Warner Computer Systems
   _____ Remote Computing
   __X__ Other (Specify) Computer Asset Management (update daily after
                             6:30 p. m. Eastern Time)
   _____ Other (Specify) _____
If data is entered via modem, what type of information is obtained? (Check all
   that apply)
   _____ Current quotes (same day)
   _____ Historical quotes (over one day old)
   __X___ Miscellaneous data used to calculate technical market
          indicators   28 items updated
   _____ Other (Specify) _____
If data is entered via modem, is dialing, log on, retrieval of required data, and
   log off automatic?   __X__ Yes   _____ No
If data is entered manually, what type of information is entered? (Check all
   that apply)
   _____ Current quotes (same day)
   _____ Historical quotes (over one day old)
   __X__ Miscellaneous data used to calculate technical market indicators
   _____ Other (Specify) _____
After data is entered, can it be easily checked and changed?
   __X__ Yes   _____ No

EXHIBIT 9–6 (*continued*)

CHARTING FEATURES

Software produces graphs on the screen in: ＿＿ Color ＿＿ Monochrome
＿X＿ Both
Graphs can be based on which data: (Check all that apply)
＿X＿ Daily ＿＿＿＿ Quarterly
＿X＿ Weekly ＿＿＿＿ Yearly
＿＿＿＿ Monthly
Maximum number of data points that can be plotted on a graph? ＿＿415＿＿
Are time periods for graphs user definable? ＿X＿ Yes ＿＿＿ No
Which of the following types of scaling are permitted? (Check all that apply)
＿X＿ Linear scaling
＿＿＿＿ Logarithmic scaling
＿＿＿＿ Semilogarithmic scaling
Is scaling automatic? ＿X＿ Yes ＿＿＿ No
Are scale ranges user definable? ＿X＿ Yes ＿＿＿ No
Can you have multiple scales? ＿＿＿ Yes ＿X＿ No
Can horizontal grid lines be drawn? ＿X＿ Yes ＿＿＿ No
Can vertical grid lines be drawn? ＿X＿ Yes ＿＿＿ No
Can customized formulas be entered for calculations and plots?
＿X＿ Yes ＿＿＿ No
Can multiple graphs be shown on an individual screen? ＿X＿ Yes ＿＿＿ No
If yes, how many? ＿＿2＿＿
Can graphs be saved on a disk? ＿＿＿ Yes ＿X＿ No
Can data used in graphs be printed in tables? ＿X＿ Yes ＿＿＿ No
Can the user "zoom in" to examine less data on the screen and "zoom out" to
examine more data on the screen? ＿X＿ Yes ＿＿＿ No
Which of the following items can be plotted?

	Yes	No
High-low-close bar charts	X	
Volume histograms	X	
Moving averages:		
Simple	X	
Weighted		X
Exponential	X	
Trend lines	X	
Trading bands		X
Oscillators		X
Support and resistance lines		X
Relative strength	X	
Cycles		X
Point & figure charts		X
Other (Specify) ＿＿＿＿＿＿＿＿＿		

EXHIBIT 9–6 (*concluded*)

TECHNICAL MARKET INDICATORS
List the technical market indicators that can be produced:

TAPE INDICATORS:
  Rate-of-change:
  Market index rate-of-change (points)
  Market index rate-of-change (percent)
  Difference of moving averages
  Relative strength index
  Modified stochastic oscillator
Advance/Decline:
  Absolute breadth index
  Advancing-declining
  Advance/decline line
  Advance/decline ratio
  Advancing issues
  Breadth thrust
  Declining issues
  McClellan oscillator
  McClellan summation index
  Overbought/oversold indicator
  STIX
  TRIN
Volume:
  Advancing volume
  Changed (A + D) volume
  Cumulative volume index
  Declining volume
  Large block ratio
  Large block trades
  Negative volume index
  On balance volume
  Positive volume index
  Upside-downside ratio
  Upside-downside volume
New Highs/Lows:
  New highs-lows
  New highs-lows cumulative
  New high/low ratio
  Number of new highs
  Number of new lows

Miscellaneous:
  Composite tape indicators
  Moving averages
  Relative strength charts

SENTIMENT INDICATORS:
  Short sales:
    Member short ratio
    Odd-lot short ratio
    Public short ratio
    Total short ratio
  Odd-lot Trades:
    Odd-lot balance index
    Odd-lot purchases
    Odd-lot sales
    Odd-lot short ratio
  Miscellaneous Sentiment:
    Composite sentiment indicators
    NYFE premium/discount
    Put/call ratio

MONETARY INDICATORS:
  Interest rates:
    Fed funds rate
    Prime rate
    13 and 26-week T bills
    Interest rate rate-of-change
    T bills spread
  Miscellaneous Monetary:
    Composite monetary indicators

OTHER INDICATORS:
  Dow Jones Industrial Average
  NYSE Composite Index
  S&P 100 (OEX)
  S&P 500 Composite Index
  Value Line Composite Index
  Rate-of-change of any indicator

OTHER FEATURES

Does the software have an autorun feature? _____ Yes __X__ No
Can you produce hard copy of all graphs? __X__ Yes _____ No
Does the software facilitate testing of trading strategies?
  __X__ Yes _____ No
        Limited

---

*N/A = not applicable.

Next, determine whether multiple charts can be shown on an individual screen. Often, it is advantageous to be able to examine charts side by side on the same screen. For example, you might want to examine the activity in two stocks or one stock and a market index, such as the Dow Jones Industrial Average, side by side.

At other times, you might want to examine a number of different technical indicators at the same time. Being able to see them all at once on the same screen makes analysis easier than having to go back and forth from one screen to another.

The ability to enter customized formulas for calculations and charting is another feature of value to the technician. With this capability you are not limited to a predefined set of indicators included in a particular package. Rather you can create indicators by entering formulas that manipulate the data the program maintains.

A "zoom" feature is also useful. This feature allows you to "zoom in" to take a closer look at a segment of a chart and "zoom out" to examine more data on the screen.

Another key capability is an autorun feature. Often, you will find yourself preparing the same charts day after day. An autorun feature enables you to define a series of charts that can be automatically prepared and printed each day. You simply enter the autorun mode and walk away from the computer. When you return later, a stack of printed charts is ready for your review. This feature can save a significant amount of your time.

Finally, the software should have the ability to specify the number of data points plotted and scale ranges, enter horizontal and vertical titles, and add horizontal and vertical grid lines.

Let's examine three technical analysis software packages and illustrate exactly what you can do with technical analysis software and your personal computer. The three packages are The Technician, MetaStock™, and CompuTrac/PC. In addition, you will find a discussion of an on-line alternative, Telescan™.

The Technician

The Technician from Computer Asset Management allows you to track and graphically display approximately 70 widely followed tape, sentiment, and monetary indicators. The Technician enables you to chart the following tape indicators: market index rate-of-change, difference of moving averages, relative strength index, modified stochastic oscillator, absolute breadth index, advancing/declining issues, advance/decline line, advance/decline ratio, advancing issues, breadth thrust, declining issues, McClellan oscillator, McClellan summation index, overbought/oversold indicator, STIX, TRIN (trading index), advancing volume, changed volume, cumulative volume index, declining volume, large block ratio, large block trades, negative volume index, on-balance volume, positive volume index, upside/downside ratio, upside/downside volume, new highs/lows, new highs/lows cumulative, new high/low ratio, number of new highs, and number of new lows.

Sentiment indicators that are available include member short ratio, odd-lot short ratio, public short ratio, total short ratio, odd-lot balance index, odd-lot purchases, odd-lot sales, New York Futures Exchange premium/discount, and put/call ratio.

Monetary indicators that can be plotted are the Fed funds rate, prime rate, 13- and 26-week Treasury bill rates, interest rate-of-change, and Treasury bills spread.

In addition, you can chart five major market indices—the Dow Jones Industrial Average, NYSE Composite Index, Standard & Poor's 100 Index (OEX), Standard & Poor's 500 Index, and Value Line Composite Index.

The first step to charting a particular indicator is to load data for a specific period. Up to 415 periods (days or weeks) of data can be examined at one time. The Technician comes with an up-to-date data disk containing data for all but five of the indicators dating back to January 1979. Data from December 1982 is provided for the remaining five indicators. This extensive data lets you use the software immediately.

After you load the data, you are ready to choose the indicator you want to chart by scrolling through a list of the indicators and pressing the return key when the desired indicator is shown between two arrows.

Next, you choose from a menu containing options for displaying the indicator. Normally, the indicator is displayed on the top half of the screen while your choice of one of the five market indices (e.g., Dow Jones Industrial Average or Standard & Poor's 500 Index) is shown on the bottom half of the screen. This allows you to visually compare changes in the indicator value to market action. Other display choices enable you to plot a volume histogram, overlay charts, and plot an indicator rate of change. You can also elect not to plot the selected indicator—for example, when you want to display the moving average of the indicator only.

Several analytical tools are available that allow you to quickly draw trend lines, parallel trend lines, support and resistance lines, vertical cycle lines, and simple and exponential moving averages. A zoom feature enables you to magnify or condense charts displayed on the screen.

Exhibit 9–7 provides a step-by-step illustration of how to chart the put/call ratio. Other indicators can be plotted just as easily.

In addition to the approximately 70 indicators tracked by The Technician, you can create up to 20 of your own custom indicators. By entering mathematical formulas you can manipulate any of the 27 data items on the data disk. Up to 10 additional data items of your choice can be manually added, plotted, and analyzed. For example, you may want to add items such as the price of a stock or the value of an index that is not already tracked by The Technician.

Data used by The Technician can be kept up-to-date manually with data from *The Wall Street Journal* and *Barron's*. However, a much easier approach is to access the Computer Asset Management on-line database. Modem updating normally takes less than one minute and can be performed on a daily basis after 6:30 P.M. (Eastern time).

To receive the maximum benefit from The Technician and similar software, you must know how to interpret the technical market indicators you chart. The Technician's user's manual helps by including a 110-page section that briefly discusses each indicator and how to interpret its results. Other software packages of this type frequently include little of such information.

The typical user should be able to learn the basic functions of a software package of this nature in a few hours. Normally, software that enables you to track technical market indicators is straightforward and easy to use.

MetaStock

Unlike The Technician with its focus on the overall market, MetaStock is designed to perform analysis of individual securities. MetaStock from Computer Asset Management offers two very unique features.

First, MetaStock gives you the capability to chart up to 1,000 data points per chart. This allows you to plot approximately four

---

EXHIBIT 9-7   Charting the Put/Call Ratio with The Technician

---

Step 1: Load program and select graphic charting from The Technician's main menu

<pre>
                          The Technician
   Last Date <3/4/86>
   ─────────────────────────────<Main Menu>──────────────

                    <G> Graphic Charting
                    <C> Custom Indicators
                    <D> Data Maintenance
                    <U> Utilities
                    <Q> Quit

                      Enter Selection...

          (C) 1984 Computer Asset Management, version 3.00
</pre>

Step 2: Load indicator data

<pre>
            LOAD DATA

     Press the [ENTER] key to continue.

  ┌───┐
  │ -> Load most recent 102 days of data   │
  │   Load most recent 205 days of data   │
  │   Load most recent 415 days of data   │
  │   Load other daily records   │
  │   │
  │   Load most recent 102 weeks of data   │
  │   Load most recent 205 weeks of data   │
  │   Load most recent 415 weeks of data   │
  │   Load other weekly records   │
  └───┘
</pre>

Step 3: Select indicator to chart

<pre>
    ┌──────────────────────────┐   ┌──────────────────────────────────────┐
    │ Odd Lot Purchases   │   │ Use the cursor control keys to select│
    │ Odd Lot Sales   │   │ the indicator you want to chart.   │
    │   │   │   │
    │   Misc. Sentiment   │   │ Press the [ENTER] key when the   │
    │   │   │ indicator is between the two arrows. │
    │ Call Volume   │   └──────────────────────────────────────┘
    │ Put Volume   │
 -> │ Put/Call Ratio   │   <-Select the Indicator to Chart
    │ NYFE Premium/Discount   │
    │   │
    │ ┌─────────────────────┐ │
    │ │ MONETARY INDICATORS │ │
    │ └─────────────────────┘ │
    │   │
    │   Interest Rates   │
    └──────────────────────────┘
</pre>

Step 4: Select display options

<pre>
              DISPLAY OPTIONS

     Press the [SPACE] bar to continue.

  ┌───┐
  │ ->   <-   │
  │   Market Index . . . . DJIA   │
  │   Volume bar chart . . . . ON   │
  │   Selected indicator . . . . ON   │
  │   NYFE futures contract . . . . OFF   │
  │   Overlay last chart . . . . OFF   │
  │   Indicator Rate-Of-Change . . . . . . OFF   │
  └───┘

              Press [F1] for Help
</pre>

EXHIBIT 9–7 (concluded)

Step 5: Generate basic chart showing indicator on top and market index on bottom

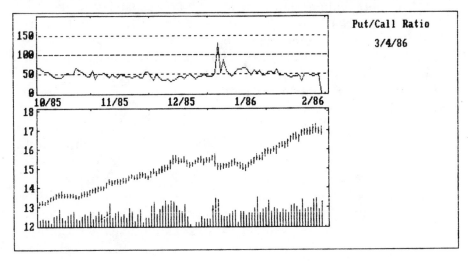

Step 6: Use analytical tools to plot moving average and trendline

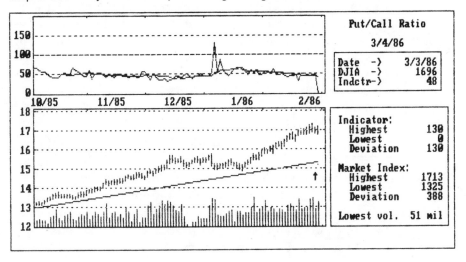

years of daily price action or 20 years of weekly prices. The ability to plot close to 20 years of weekly prices is particularly valuable for cycle analysis.

A second unique feature is MetaStock's capability to display from 1 to 36 charts on the screen at one time. Charts can be generated in over 35 different sizes ranging from 1 inch by 1 1/2 inches to full-screen size. This feature is particularly beneficial since you can generate a variety of technical indicators and display all of the results on the screen at one time instead of examining only one indicator at a time.

The chart analysis section of MetaStock provides access to a variety of sophisticated technical indicators including price and volume trend, price rate-of-change, stochastic oscillator, price difference of averages, accumulation/distribution, Chaiken accumulation/distribution oscillator, relative strength index, on-balance volume, volume rate-of-change, volume difference of averages, volume line, positive volume indicator, and negative volume indicator.

To use MetaStock, you first obtain the data necessary for analyses. This data can pertain to stocks, bonds, mutual funds, options, indices, or commodities. Data can be entered manually using the data maintenance section of the system, but an on-line service is faster. Data can be maintained in CompuTrac, Dow Jones, or CSI format and can be retrieved from Commodity Systems, Inc. (CSI), CompuServe, Dow Jones News/Retrieval, Interactive Data Corporation, National Computer Network, Remote Computing, and Warner Computer Systems (see Chapter 11 for more information on data retrieval).

Once you have data for the securities you want to analyze, you are ready to load a specific data file into the computer's memory. MetaStock lists the data files from which you select the security you want to chart on your data disk. The system asks the number of periods of data you want to load. Up to 1,000 periods of data can be loaded at one time. After loading the data, a bar chart of the historical prices appears on the screen.

You can select a particular indicator through the indicator menu by simply pressing the key shown to its left in the menu. In some cases, you will be asked for additional information after you select a particular indicator. For example, if you press F3 (function key number three) for stochastic oscillator, you will be asked for the number of periods you want to use in the calculation.

After charting a particular security or an indicator, you may choose to utilize some of MetaStock's analytical tools. These tools enable you to draw trendlines, parallel trend lines, support and resistance lines, linear regression lines, and vertical cycle lines.

In addition, by accessing the moving average menu you can draw an unlimited number of moving averages. The moving averages can be simple, weighted, or exponential, and can be shifted vertically or horizontally.

Exhibit 9–8 provides a step-by-step example of using Meta-Stock. For illustrative purposes, historical pricing data for IBM has been plotted along with a number of indicators.

CompuTrac/PC

CompuTrac/PC from CompuTrac, Inc., is a technical analysis software package targeted at active traders of stocks and commodities. It offers the capability to perform a wide range of very sophisticated technical studies.

When you buy CompuTrac/PC, you actually become a member of a group, the Technical Analysis Group, rather than merely purchasing a piece of software for a one-time fee. Your feedback is welcome and results in updates in the software that you receive. Since its inception, the Technical Analysis Group's goal has been to blend the best thoughts of serious traders into CompuTrac/PC, thus perpetually enhancing its value over time.

The basic philosophy behind CompuTrac/PC is that all traders work differently because of their personalities, amount of capital available, and numerous other factors. CompuTrac/PC is set up as a "toolbag of technical analysis tools." You are not expected to use all of the technical studies and tools available, but only those which best fit your individual style of trading.

CompuTrac/PC is divided into six primary sections: Analysis, System Automation, Data Base Maintenance, System Constants, User Study Editor, and Profitability Editor.

Analysis is the section of the system in which you will spend most of your time. Through the Analysis section, you have access to a variety of sophisticated technical studies including advance-decline, Bolton-Tremblay, commodity channel index, commodity selection index, demand index, detrend, directional movement, HAL momentum index, Haurlan index, linear regression, Mc-Clellan oscillator, median price, momentum, moving average,

EXHIBIT 9–8   Charting IBM and Various Technical Indicators with MetaStock

Step 1: Load program and select security to be charted

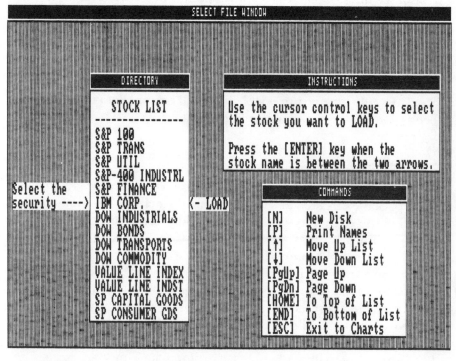

Step 2: Load price and volume data for the security

```
                 LOAD NUMBER

There are  281 records in this file.

Enter first record to load -->      1
Enter last record to load  -->    281
Enter compression factor (1)->?
```

EXHIBIT 9–8 (*concluded*)

Step 3: Generate basic high-low-close bar chart with volume histogram

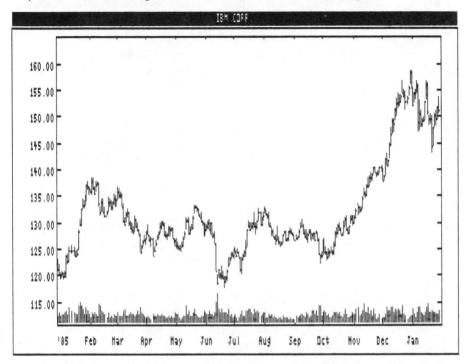

Step 4: Plot various technical indicators and add moving average line, trendline, etc.

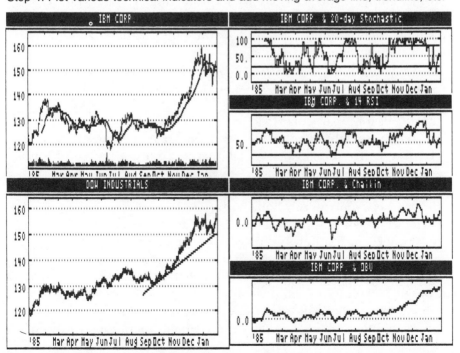

moving average convergence/divergence, on-balance volume, open interest, oscillator, parabolic, point and figure, rate of change, ratio, relative strength index, Schultz A/T, short-term trading index, spread, stockastic (K%D), swing index, volatility, volume accumulation, volume accumulation oscillator, volume histogram, weighted close, and Williams % R.

Most of these technical studies are very sophisticated, and proper interpretation of their results requires a working knowledge of the particular study. CompuTrac/PC's user's manual includes a 65-page section that briefly discusses each study and how to interpret its results. In addition, reference sources are noted for anyone who wants a more thorough understanding.

The various operations included in Analysis can be easily performed through the use of function keys. These are the keys on the left-hand side of the computer's keyboard labeled F1 through F10. CompuTrac/PC uses these keys so that most operations can be completed with just one, two or three keystrokes.

Normally, you first press F3 to load a data file into the computer's memory. After loading a specific data file, you press the F1 key twice to access a menu of the available studies. Pressing the alphabetic character located to the left of the study's name would lead you to a series of questions for that particular study. For example, if you select choice 0 for moving average, you would be asked if you want a simple, weighted, or exponential moving average, the period of the average you want calculated, and if you want the average centered or not.

Pressing the F6 key will lead you to a submenu of analytical tools that allow you to draw trendlines, parallel trendlines, and envelopes; perform cycle analysis; determine the amount of retracement for a particular field; compress data from daily to weekly or weekly to monthly format; and perform several specialized charting conventions, such as Fibonacci fan lines, arcs, and time zones.

Other function keys enable you to switch the area of graphic display between the top half, bottom half, and full screen, print various types of output, and magnify or condense charts displayed on the screen. Exhibit 9–9 provides a step-by-step illustration of a typical session using the Analysis section of CompuTrac/PC.

Once you familiarize yourself with the Analysis section of CompuTrac/PC, you will probably find that you want to perform the same operations day after day. Using the system's Task Editor and Schedule Utilities, you can enter which operations you want

EXHIBIT 9–9 Charting IBM and Various Technical Studies with CompuTrac/PC

Step 1: Load program and select analysis from the main menu

```
01-29-1986              C O M P U - T R A C   P C            00:01:43
                            VERSION  2.32

                        MAIN MENU - <esc> to Exit

A - Analysis
B - System Automation
C - Data base maintenance
D - System constants
E - User Study Editor
F - Profitablity Editor

Your choice: A




                        Expires: 861231
        Video      Ram-K  Drives: Floppy Hard     Ports: Comm Parallel      DOS
  Hires monitor    256            2     None              1       1        2.10
```

Step 2: Press F3 (function key number 3) to obtain list of data files

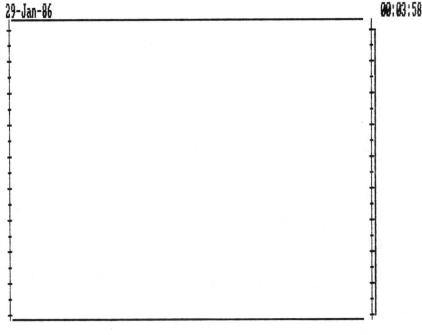

EXHIBIT 9–9 *(continued)*

Step 3: Select data file

```
                        ITEM SELECTION - NEW                    00:05:42
                           <esc> to Exit

A - Change diskettes              N - SP CAPITAL GOODS
B - S&P 100                       O - SP CONSUMER GDS
C - S&P TRANS                     P - Windsor Fund
D - S&P UTIL                      Q - UM-Mutual Shares
E - S&P-400 INDUSTRL
F - S&P FINANCE
G - IBM CORP.
H - DOW INDUSTRIALS
I - DOW BONDS
J - DOW TRANSPORTS
K - DOW COMMODITY
L - VALUE LINE INDEX
M - VALUE LINE INDST

Your choice: A
```

Step 4: Plot basic high-low-close bar chart

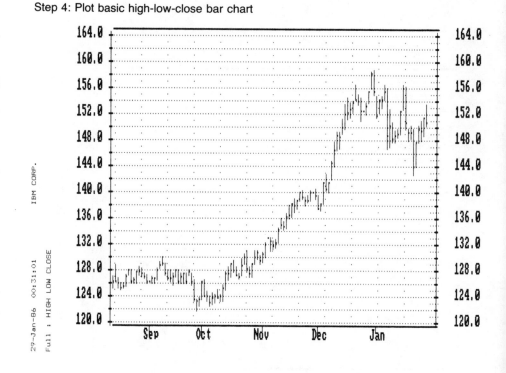

EXHIBIT 9–9 (continued)

Step 5: Choose technical studies from study selection menu

```
                          STUDY SELECTION                    00:09:32
                          <esc> to Exit
                          Pg: 1 of 2

A - Advance-Decline              N - Momentum
B - Bolton-Tremblay              O - Moving Average
C - Commodity Channel Index      P - Open Interest
D - Commodity Selection Index    Q - Oscillator
E - Demand Index                 R - Parabolic (SAR)
F - Detrend                      S - Point & Figure
G - Directional Movement         T - Rate of Change
H - Hal Momentum                 U - Ratio
I - Haurlan Index                V - Relative Strength Index
J - Linear Regression            W - Schultz A/T
K - MA Convergence/Divergence    X - Short Term Trading Index
L - McClellan Oscillator         Y - Spread
M - Median Price                 Z - Stochastic (K%D)

Your choice: A

                          PgDn for more
```

Step 6: Plot 21-day moving average and trading bands 2.5 percent above and below the 21-day moving average

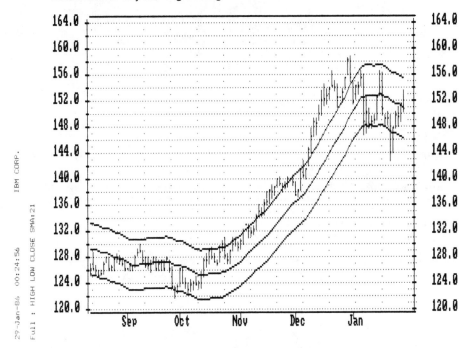

EXHIBIT 9–9 *(concluded)*

Step 7: Plot 20-day stochastic study on top of screen and volume histogram with 20-day moving average on bottom of screen

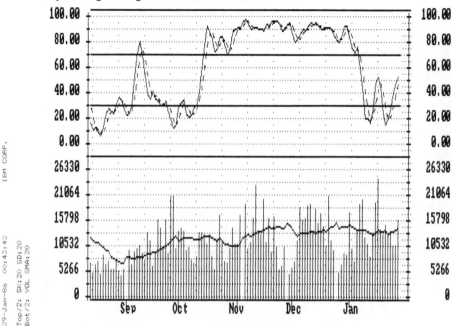

performed and indicate on which data so the computer can automatically perform all of your routine work. For example, you could set up a series of 10 technical studies to be performed automatically each day. Press a few keys, and you can walk away from your computer and return later to examine the results produced on your printer.

CompuTrac/PC can use data pertaining to stocks, bonds, options, indices, or commodities. Data can be entered manually using the Data Base Maintenance section of the system, although it is recommended that you use one of the on-line services. On-line services from which you can retrieve data include Commodity Systems, Inc., Interactive Data Corporation, National Computer Network, QFS, Inc., Remote Computing, I.P. Sharp Associates, and Warner Computer Systems (see Chapter 11 for more information on data retrieval).

The User Study Editor allows you to augment the studies incorporated in CompuTrac/PC with studies you have devised yourself or obtained from other sources. This is basically a programming subsystem that provides you with the means to perform the particular study in which you are interested.

The Profitability Editor is one of CompuTrac/PC's most useful features. It enables you to test trading systems for profitability over time. This capability is discussed in greater detail in Chapter 10.

CompuTrac/PC is one of the most sophisticated technical analysis software packages available. With it you can easily perform very complex technical analysis studies on an ongoing basis.

Telescan—An On-Line Alternative

In order to use a technical analysis software package like MetaStock or CompuTrac/PC to plot even a simple chart, you must first manually enter daily price and volume data or retrieve it from an on-line service. The quickest method is to use an on-line service, but retrieving only one year of data takes several minutes even with a service, and then you have to wait for the data to be plotted. With these software packages you are limited by time, the length of the period for which data can be plotted, and the cost of retrieving data from an on-line service.

Telescan from Telescan, Inc., offers a unique alternative to these packages. Using the Telescan Analyzer software package and a personal computer, you can access Telescan's on-line database and retrieve charts depicting up to 12 years of data for over 7,000 stocks and 150 market indices (including Standard & Poor's industry groups). For each stock, you can graphically display price and volume data for from one month to 12 years, moving averages, cycles, momentum, on-balance volume, relative strength, trendlines, book value, dividends, earnings, cash flow, capital spending, inflation adjustment, insider trading, and short interest.

Rather than retrieving one day's data at a time and then plotting it on the screen, Telescan Analyzer retrieves and displays a complete chart for the period you request. As a result, each chart can be retrieved quickly, usually in less than 20 seconds—10 to 20 percent of the time it would take using a normal technical analysis software package.

Telescan Analyzer is simple to use. After signing on to the Telescan database, you simply enter a stock's ticker symbol or the partial or full name of the stock you want to view, wait for the screen to clear, and, in a matter of seconds, a chart of the stock you selected appears.

To change time spans, you simply press any of the numerical keys 1 to 0 to display the corresponding number of years of data (1 to 10 years) or press the function key corresponding to the number of months of data you want. Since the Telescan database contains information dating back to January 1973, you can display the maximum data for a stock by pressing the equal (=) key.

Menus are displayed adjacent to the stock graphs at all times. They list the keys you need to press for each available feature. From the Main Menu you can select six technical indicators: moving average, cycle analysis, momentum, on-balance volume, relative strength, and trendline marker. Six fundamental indicators can be used to analyze stocks: book value, dividends, earnings, cash flow, capital spending, and a composite of these five fundamental indicators. Three additional indicators that can be chosen from the Main Menu are adjustment for inflation, insider trading, and short interest.

Telescan Analyzer allows you to plot one or two moving averages of whatever length you specify. These can be either standard or exponential moving averages. You can also graph the difference between a moving average and the closing price, or the difference between two moving averages.

When you choose the cycle analysis feature, Telescan displays the stock chart with a sine curve overlayed. Using the various arrow and function keys, the sine curve can be expanded, contracted, moved up, down, left or right until it best fits the cycle of price movements. Telescan will identify the period of the cycle and the dates for the next cycle top and bottom.

A momentum indicator for the time interval that you specify can be plotted at the bottom of the screen. An on-balance volume chart for the stock of your choice can be obtained by simply pressing one key from the Main Menu.

Telescan also allows you to compare a stock with the Dow Jones Industrial Average, New York Stock Exchange Index, American Stock Exchange Index, NASDAQ Index, its own industry group, or another stock.

Finally, Telescan easily creates trendlines. Using the arrow keys, you move a marker left, right, up, and down to mark the two points you choose. A press of a function key draws the trendline between. Parallel trendlines can be drawn as well.

Exhibit 9–10 provides a step-by-step sample session using Telescan Analyzer. Telescan offers you the capability to retrieve

EXHIBIT 9–10   Charting Eastman Kodak with Telescan Analyzer

Step 1: Select stock graphs from the on-line menu

TELESCAN

```
ON-LINE MENU


1. WHATS NEW
2. STOCK GRAPHS
3. AUTO-RUN
4. EXIT DATABASE


ENTER NUMBER OF CHOICE:
```

(C) Copyright 1983 TELESCAN INC - All rights Reserved

Step 2: Enter the stock symbol (EK) and generate a 12-year bar chart

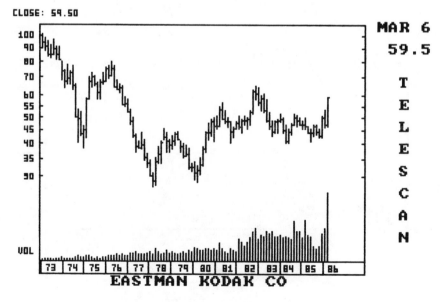

EXHIBIT 9–10 *(concluded)*

Step 3: Press F6 (Function Key Number 6) to plot a six-month bar chart

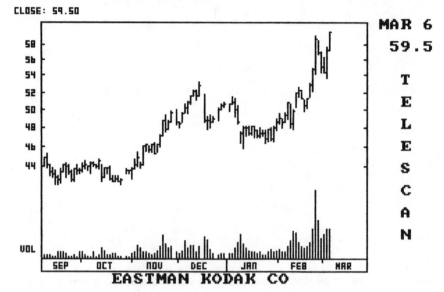

Step 4: Add a 20-day moving average line and momentum indicator

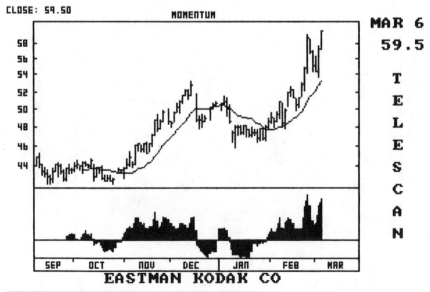

SOURCE: By permission of Telescan, Inc.

and analyze graphic information quickly and easily. If you need a quick chart or plan to perform only simple technical analysis, Telescan Analyzer may be exactly what you are looking for. However, Telescan Analyzer lacks many of the sophisticated analytical tools offered by technical analysis software packages, such as MetaStock and CompuTrac/PC. Keep your specific needs in mind when making your choice.

A Warning

One warning—while technical analysis software packages do facilitate the process of chart preparation, don't expect them to replace the human brain. You still have to interpret the charts and decide what to buy or sell and when to do so. Furthermore, the publishers of technical analysis software packages normally assume that users already have a good working knowledge of technical analysis methods and techniques. The software is not designed to teach technical analysis but to provide a framework in which you can perform technical analysis faster and more accurately. If you are new to technical analysis, read a few good books on the subject before purchasing a technical analysis software package.

CONCLUSION

Whether you are analyzing the overall stock market or looking at an individual security, preparing bar charts and indicator charts, as well as using chart analysis tools, is extremely time-consuming if done manually. Fortunately, by using a personal computer and technical analysis software, you can solve that problem, leaving more time for studying the charts and making the best possible investment decisions. Use the technical analysis software packages illustrated in this chapter as a guide to what you can expect to do with technical analysis software. They fully utilize the speed and graphics capabilities of the personal computer and contain the latest technical indicators available.

CHAPTER 10

Testing Trading Strategies

For years, we have been told that computers can be used to test various theories and strategies. And, in fact, many stock brokerage firms have been using large computers for years in an attempt to identify profitable stock market trading strategies.

But what about individual investors? Can they use personal computers to test their stock market trading strategies? The answer is yes, with software such as CompuTrac/PC from CompuTrac, Inc., and ProfitTaker from Investment Growth Corporation.

COMPUTRAC/PC

As discussed in Chapter 9, CompuTrac/PC allows investors to perform a variety of stock market analyses, but perhaps its most useful and powerful feature is its ability to test trading strategies over time. A CompuTrac/PC profitability test allows you to simulate trading activity with historical price data, using price levels and technical study result levels to trigger entry into and exit from market positions. Your trading rules dictate the conditions for entry and exit into long or short positions. The performance of your trading system is then measured over historical data for profitability.

To maximize the use of a profitability test, you can choose an optimized mode so that the same test can be applied to varying periods and condition values. The best and therefore most profitable combination of periods and condition values can then be easily isolated.

For example, suppose you want to test a moving average crossover system on a specific stock. Assume that two moving averages are used and a buy signal is given when the shorter term moving average crosses from below to above the longer term moving average. A sell signal is given when the shorter term moving average crosses from above to below the longer term moving average.

Using CompuTrac/PC, you can instruct the computer to examine each combination of moving averages between, say, 2 and 50, and produce an optimization report showing which pair of moving averages will yield the greatest profit given the fewest number of trades. This capability allows you to test various theories before any money is actually committed to the market.

A summary of the steps taken to create a typical profitability test follows:

Step 1—Enter a name for the profitability test.

Step 2—Decide whether to optimize certain parameters within the profitability test.

Step 3—Enter the names of data fields that will be used in the profitability test. For example, the open, high, low, and closing prices, simple moving average, and so forth.

Step 4—Select which reports of test results you want printed. Four reports are available. A summary report, as illustrated in Exhibit 10–1, provides summary information such as best trade, worst trade, total number of trades, number of profitable trades, number of losing trades, and gross profit or loss. A trades report provides one line of key information for each date that a trade is closed throughout the profitability test. A third report produces one line of key information for each date that a trade is open. And the final report generates a line of key information for each date whether there is trading activity or not (see Exhibit 10–2).

Step 5—Decide whether to save certain test results for charting purposes.

Step 6—Since commission charges can have a dramatic effect on your trading profits, provision is made at this point to enter a commission per trade amount.

Step 7—Similarly, an amount for slippage can be entered. Slippage is the difference between the price at which your trading system indicates to enter or exit a position and the price when the order is actually executed.

Step 8—Optionally, enter an initial position, long or short, at a specified date and price.

EXHIBIT 10–1   Sample Profit/Loss Summary Report from CompuTrac/PC
Profitability Test

29-Jan-86 00:25:55	IBM CORP.	> MATEST.PFT	Page: 7

```
------------------------------------- Profit / Loss - Summary -----------------------------------------

      Item                        Long              Short                 Net
--------------------------------------- Per Trade Ranges ------------------------------------

Best Trade                        20.9               4.9                 20.9
..Date                          860108            850412               860108
Worst Trade                       -5.1              -7.1                 -7.1
..Date                          860117            860116               860116
Max Open P/L                      30.3               9.9                 30.3
..Date                          851230            850613               851230
Min Open P/L                      -0.8              -3.8                 -3.8
..Date                          860129            860115               860115
------------------------------------- Overall Ranges ------------------------------------

Max P/L                           17.6              10.5                 17.6
..Date                          860108            860116               860108
Min P/L                           -2.1              -3.3                 -3.3
..Date                          850306            951014               851014
Max Equity                        27.0              18.0                 27.0
..Date                          851230            860110               851230
Min Equity                        -3.8              -3.0                 -3.8
..Date                          851021            850606               851021
----------------------------------------- Statistics -----------------------------------------

Periods                            147               108                  255
Trades                              12                12                   24
# Profitable                         3                 3                    6
# Losing                             9                 9                   18
% Profitable                     25.00             25.00                25.00
% Losing                         75.00             75.00                75.00
------------------------------------------ Results ----------------------------------------

Commission                         0.0               0.0                  0.0
Slippage                           0.0               0.0                  0.0
Gross P/L                         10.6              -6.1                  4.5
Open P/L                          -0.8               0.0                 -0.8
P/L                               10.6              -6.1                  4.5
Equity                             9.9              -6.1                  3.8
```

Step 9—Enter the conditions for taking a long position (buying)—for example, when the shorter term moving average crosses above the longer term moving average.

Step 10—Indicate the price at which the long position should be taken. The position can be taken on the closing price of the day the conditions are met or the opening price on the following day.

Step 11—Enter the conditions for exiting a long position (selling)—for example, when the shorter term moving average crosses below the longer term moving average.

Step 12—Indicate the price at which the long position should be closed (sold).

Step 13—Enter the conditions for a stop-loss filter. For example, if the price declines by 15 percent from the entry price, exit the long position.

EXHIBIT 10–2 Sample Detail Report from CompuTrac/PC Profitability Test

```
29-Jan-86  00:24:03              IBM CORP.              > MATEST.PFT      Page:   5
```

Date	Time S/L	Entry Date	Entry Time	Entry Price	Exit/ Last	Max P/L	Min P/L	Gross P/L	Net P/L	Max Equity	Min Equity	Equity
851016	N/A L	851014	N/A	128.0	129.4	1.4	0.0	1.4	1.4	8.1	-3.3	-1.9
851017	N/A L	851014	N/A	128.0	128.5	1.4	0.0	0.5	0.5	8.1	-3.3	-2.8
851018	N/A L	851014	N/A	128.0	127.6	1.4	-0.4	-0.4	-0.4	8.1	-3.6	-3.6
851021	N/A L	851014	N/A	128.0	127.5	1.4	-0.5	-0.5	-0.5	8.1	-3.8	-3.8
851022	N/A L	851014	N/A	128.0	129.1	1.4	-0.5	1.1	1.1	8.1	-3.8	-2.1
851023	N/A L	851014	N/A	128.0	130.5	2.5	-0.5	2.5	2.5	8.1	-3.8	-0.8
851024	N/A L	851014	N/A	128.0	128.6	2.5	-0.5	0.6	0.6	8.1	-3.8	-2.6
851025	N/A L	851014	N/A	128.0	128.0	2.5	-0.5	0.0	0.0	8.1	-3.8	-3.3
851028	N/A L	851014	N/A	128.0	129.4	2.5	-0.5	1.4	1.4	8.1	-3.8	-1.9
851029	N/A L	851014	N/A	128.0	130.5	2.5	-0.5	2.5	2.5	8.1	-3.8	-0.8
851030	N/A L	851014	N/A	128.0	131.1	3.1	-0.5	3.1	3.1	8.1	-3.8	-0.1
851031	N/A L	851014	N/A	128.0	129.9	3.1	-0.5	1.9	1.9	8.1	-3.8	-1.4
851101	N/A L	851014	N/A	128.0	130.9	3.1	-0.5	2.9	2.9	8.1	-3.8	-0.4
851104	N/A L	851014	N/A	128.0	132.3	4.3	-0.5	4.3	4.3	8.1	-3.8	1.0
851105	N/A L	851014	N/A	128.0	133.4	5.4	-0.5	5.4	5.4	8.1	-3.8	2.1
851106	N/A L	851014	N/A	128.0	132.9	5.4	-0.5	4.9	4.9	8.1	-3.8	1.6
851107	N/A L	851014	N/A	128.0	132.1	5.4	-0.5	4.1	4.1	8.1	-3.8	0.9
851108	N/A L	851014	N/A	128.0	132.5	5.4	-0.5	4.5	4.5	8.1	-3.8	1.3
851111	N/A L	851014	N/A	128.0	134.6	6.6	-0.5	6.6	6.6	8.1	-3.8	3.4
851112	N/A L	851014	N/A	128.0	135.4	7.4	-0.5	7.4	7.4	8.1	-3.8	4.1
851113	N/A L	851014	N/A	128.0	135.0	7.4	-0.5	7.0	7.0	8.1	-3.8	3.8
851114	N/A L	851014	N/A	128.0	136.6	8.6	-0.5	8.6	8.6	8.1	-3.8	5.4
851115	N/A L	851014	N/A	128.0	136.8	8.8	-0.5	8.8	8.8	8.1	-3.8	5.5
851118	N/A L	851014	N/A	128.0	138.5	10.5	-0.5	10.5	10.5	8.1	-3.8	7.3
851119	N/A L	851014	N/A	128.0	138.3	10.5	-0.5	10.3	10.3	8.1	-3.8	7.0
851120	N/A L	851014	N/A	128.0	139.0	11.0	-0.5	11.0	11.0	8.1	-3.8	7.8
851121	N/A L	851014	N/A	128.0	140.3	12.3	-0.5	12.3	12.3	9.0	-3.8	9.0
851122	N/A L	851014	N/A	128.0	139.5	12.3	-0.5	11.5	11.5	9.0	-3.8	8.3
851125	N/A L	851014	N/A	128.0	139.0	12.3	-0.5	11.0	11.0	9.0	-3.8	7.8
851126	N/A L	851014	N/A	128.0	139.0	12.3	-0.5	11.0	11.0	9.0	-3.8	7.8
851127	N/A L	851014	N/A	128.0	140.3	12.3	-0.5	12.3	12.3	9.0	-3.8	9.0
851128	N/A L	851014	N/A	128.0	140.3	12.3	-0.5	12.3	12.3	9.0	-3.8	9.0
851129	N/A L	851014	N/A	128.0	139.8	12.3	-0.5	11.8	11.8	9.0	-3.8	8.5
851202	N/A L	851014	N/A	128.0	137.9	12.3	-0.5	9.9	9.9	9.0	-3.8	6.6
851203	N/A L	851014	N/A	128.0	138.6	12.3	-0.5	10.6	10.6	9.0	-3.8	7.4
851204	N/A L	851014	N/A	128.0	141.9	13.9	-0.5	13.9	13.9	10.6	-3.8	10.6
851205	N/A L	851014	N/A	128.0	140.8	13.9	-0.5	12.8	12.8	10.6	-3.8	9.5
851206	N/A L	851014	N/A	128.0	141.8	13.9	-0.5	13.8	13.8	10.6	-3.8	10.5
851209	N/A L	851014	N/A	128.0	144.6	16.6	-0.5	16.6	16.6	13.4	-3.8	13.4
851210	N/A L	851014	N/A	128.0	146.6	18.6	-0.5	18.6	18.6	15.4	-3.8	15.4
851211	N/A L	851014	N/A	128.0	149.0	21.0	-0.5	21.0	21.0	17.8	-3.8	17.8
851212	N/A L	851014	N/A	128.0	148.6	21.0	-0.5	20.6	20.6	17.8	-3.8	17.4
851213	N/A L	851014	N/A	128.0	150.3	22.3	-0.5	22.3	22.3	19.0	-3.8	19.0
851216	N/A L	851014	N/A	128.0	152.3	24.3	-0.5	24.3	24.3	21.0	-3.8	21.0
851217	N/A L	851014	N/A	128.0	152.5	24.5	-0.5	24.5	24.5	21.3	-3.8	21.3
851218	N/A L	851014	N/A	128.0	152.9	24.9	-0.5	24.9	24.9	21.6	-3.8	21.6
851219	N/A L	851014	N/A	128.0	153.8	25.8	-0.5	25.8	25.8	22.5	-3.8	22.5
851220	N/A L	851014	N/A	128.0	154.3	26.3	-0.5	26.3	26.3	23.0	-3.8	23.0
851223	N/A L	851014	N/A	128.0	154.0	26.3	-0.5	26.0	26.0	23.0	-3.8	22.8
851224	N/A L	851014	N/A	128.0	152.8	26.3	-0.5	24.8	24.8	23.0	-3.8	21.5

Step 14—Indicate the price at which a stop-loss for the long position should be executed—for example, the opening price on the day after the price declines by more than 15 percent from the entry price.

Step 15—Enter the conditions for a short position (selling), such as when the shorter term moving average crosses below the longer term moving average.

Step 16—Indicate the price at which the short position should be taken.

Step 17—Enter the conditions for exiting a short position (buying)—for example, when the shorter term moving average crosses above the longer term moving average.

Step 18—Indicate the price at which the short position should be closed (bought).

Step 19—Enter the conditions for a stop-loss filter on a short position.

Step 20—Indicate the price at which a stop-loss for the short position should be executed.

The conditions you specify can be as complex or simple as you wish. But, as you can see, CompuTrac/PC has the capability to account for all of the factors that would affect an actual trade. Therefore, the results of a profitability test can be used as a simulation of the actual results that would have occurred.

Of course, the fact that a trading strategy would have been successful in the past doesn't guarantee that it will continue to be successful. Nonetheless, the profitability testing feature is extremely helpful in eliminating unsuccessful trading strategies and fine-tuning successful ones.

PROFITTAKER

Additional testing of trading strategies can be performed using ProfitTaker, which is geared toward active commodity and futures traders. As with CompuTrac/PC, ProfitTaker gives full consideration to all of the factors that can affect an actual trade (such as commissions, slippage, etc.).

ProfitTaker has two main parts: ProfitAnalyst and ProfitTaker. ProfitAnalyst is a history tester that allows you to simulate real-time trading. It lets you test and customize your trading strategy and determine the best technical indicators that are employed by ProfitTaker during day-to-day trading.

ProfitAnalyst allows you to determine the optimum value of any combination of the seven technical indicators used by ProfitTaker. The seven technical indicators include a timing filter, short-term directional indicator, long-term directional indicator, and long and short sensitivity bands for stop-loss and re-entry purposes.

Four reports can be generated during the process of historical simulation. As illustrated in Exhibit 10–3, the trading history report provides a day-by-day accounting of the test results. The trading signals report displays the execution dates when the system entered and exited the market (bought or sold), the execution prices, profits and losses on closed out trades, number of consecutive losing trades, maximum dollars of consecutive losing trades, and the cumulative net equity. The third report provides a concise summary of the simulated trading results (see Exhibit 10–4). And, the final report displays information on the optimized values of the technical indicators.

After determining the optimum values for the technical indicators using ProfitAnalyst, you then turn to ProfitTaker, which uses the optimum values to generate specific buy and sell signals on a daily basis. These signals can be used as a basis for actual trading of a specific futures contract.

CONCLUSION

The value of testing trading strategies using historical data should not be underestimated. In the past, investors have traded securities on paper for a short time before actually investing their money. Now that process has been improved. You can test hundreds of trading strategies over years of historical data with little effort using your personal computer.

EXHIBIT 10–3 Sample ProfitAnalyst Trading History Report

```
                     ProfitAnalyst Trading History
                       System Date [07-08-1984]
History Test For: [COMEX GOLD]  Source Drive [A:]  Date Drive [B:]  Page: 1
Entr=Close  Exit=Close  Ranges:  TF=3  SD=5  LD=18   LS/Band=.03   SS/Band=.03
               >>>> PRICE HISTORY <<<<   >> INDICATORS <<    >TRADING POSITION
```

Rec	Date	Open	High	Low	Close	TF	SD	LD	Signal	No Change
1	02-01-82	3870	3900	3853	3892	0	0	0		Sideways
2	02-02-82	3869	3895	3845	3847	0	0	0		Sideways
3	02-03-82	3865	3873	3852	3868	3869	0	0		Sideways
4	02-04-82	3910	3945	3910	3938	3884	0	0		Sideways
5	02-05-82	3920	3926	3892	3920	3909	3893	0		Sideways
6	02-08-82	3880	3890	3853	3868	3909	3888	0		Sideways
7	02-09-82	3845	3879	3840	3876	3888	3894	0		Sideways
8	02-10-82	3900	3920	3883	3913	3886	3903	0		Sideways
9	02-11-82	3870	3887	3827	3840	3876	3883	0		Sideways
10	02-12-82	3835	3859	3830	3849	3867	3869	0		Sideways
11	02-16-82	3820	3828	3793	3818	3836	3859	0		Sideways
12	02-17-82	3820	3825	3786	3811	3826	3846	0		Sideways
13	02-18-82	3745	3759	3739	3741	3798	3812	0		Sideways
14	02-19-82	3750	3753	3685	3693	3748	3782	0		Sideways
15	02-22-82	3680	3713	3670	3688	3707	3750	0		Sideways
16	02-23-82	3660	3685	3627	3677	3686	3722	0		Sideways
17	02-24-82	3690	3728	3666	3724	3696	3705	0		Sideways
18	02-25-82	3710	3731	3682	3698	3700	3696	3815		Sideways
19	02-26-82	3670	3677	3640	3645	3689	3686	3801	Entr Shrt	
20	03-01-82	3625	3663	3625	3658	3667	3680	3790		Stay Shrt
21	03-02-82	3665	3665	3602	3616	3640	3668	3776		Stay Shrt
22	03-03-82	3580	3585	3535	3542	3605	3632	3754		Stay Shrt
23	03-04-82	3515	3525	3455	3468	3542	3586	3729		Stay Shrt
24	03-05-82	3430	3466	3360	3363	3458	3529	3701		Stay Shrt
25	03-08-82	3350	3350	3230	3310	3380	3460	3670		Stay Shrt
26	03-09-82	3285	3365	3268	3360	3344	3409	3639		Stay Shrt
27	03-10-82	3370	3400	3328	3388	3353	3378	3614		Stay Shrt
28	03-11-82	3350	3360	3295	3300	3349	3344	3583		Stay Shrt
29	03-12-82	3240	3260	3175	3196	3295	3311	3549		Stay Shrt
30	03-15-82	3170	3270	3125	3262	3253	3301	3518		Stay Shrt
31	03-16-82	3230	3280	3140	3145	3201	3258	3485		Stay Shrt
32	03-17-82	3165	3215	3137	3193	3200	3219	3457		Stay Shrt
33	03-18-82	3253	3260	3208	3252	3197	3210	3433		Stay Shrt
34	03-19-82	3160	3200	3145	3177	3207	3206	3405		Stay Shrt
35	03-22-82	3225	3252	3203	3246	3225	3203	3379	Covr Shrt	

```
************************************************************************
                   ROLLOVER INTO: COMEX GOLD 06/82
************************************************************************
```

Rec	Date	Open	High	Low	Close	TF	SD	LD	Signal	No Change
67	03-22-82	3300	3323	3275	3316	3296	3273	3452	Entr Shrt	
68	03-23-82	3380	3400	3330	3339	3301	3298	3428		Stay Shrt
69	03-24-82	3410	3425	3387	3412	3356	3328	3410		Stay Shrt
70	03-25-82	3340	3360	3310	3336	3362	3330	3388		Stay Shrt
71	03-26-82	3297	3318	3280	3292	3347	3339	3366		Stay Shrt
72	03-29-82	3255	3310	3234	3305	3311	3337	3348		Stay Shrt
73	03-30-82	3315	3334	3260	3265	3287	3322	3333		Stay Shrt
74	03-31-82	3270	3350	3258	3342	3304	3308	3328		Stay Shrt
75	04-02-82	3350	3372	3321	3368	3346	3322	3321	**Trnd-Rv	

EXHIBIT 10-4 Sample ProfitAnalyst Summary Report

```
                    ProfitAnalyst Summary
                    System Date [07-08-1984]
History Test for: [T. Bills]    Source Drive[A:]    Data Drive[B:]    Page:1
Entr=Open  Exit=Open    Ranges:  TF=4  SD=9  LD=18   LS/Band=.00  SS/Band=.00
                    Trading Performance Results
---------------------------------------------------------------------------
Total Closed Out Trades...............................      7
Long Winning Trades...................................      4
Short Winning Trades..................................      0
Total Winning Trades..................................      4
Long Losing Trades....................................      1
Short Losing Trades...................................      2
Total Losing Trades...................................      3
Total Breakeven Trades................................      0

% Winning Trades......................................   0.572
% Losing Trades.......................................   0.428
% Breakeven Trades....................................      0

Total Realized Profits................................  17,725
Total Realized Losses................................. -3,075
Cumulative Profit or Loss.............................  14,650
Ratio Cumulative Profit to Total Realized Losses......   4.764

Maximum Winning Trade.................................   7,975
Maximum Losing Trade.................................. -2,300
Average Winning Trade.................................   4,431.000
Average Losing Trade.................................. -1,025.000
Ratio Average Winning to Losing Trade.................   4.323

Average Profit or Loss per Trade......................   2,093.000

Max Number Consecutive Losing Trades..................      2
Max Dollars Consecutive Loss.......................... -2,325
Max Drawdown- Closed Out Trades....................... -2,325

Profit Factor.........................................   5.764
Sharpe Ratio..........................................   0.059
T. Bill Rate..........................................   0.090
Leverage Factor.......................................   0.050
Commissions Factor....................................  75.000
Slippage Factor.......................................  75.000

Commissions - Closed Out Trades.......................    525
Execution Slippage....................................    525
Cumulative Net Realized Profit or Loss................  13,600
Ratio Comm and Slip to Cum Net Realized Profit........   0.075

Total Unrealized Profits on Open Trade................     75
Total Unrealized Losses on Open Trade.................      0

Total Days in File(s).................................    509
Total Rollovers.......................................      3
Conversion Factor.....................................      2
Converted Point Value.................................  12.500
Converted Daily Limit.................................    150
```

CHAPTER 11

Retrieving Historical Pricing Information

Most technical analysis software that has been discussed requires the input of extensive historical pricing information in order to prepare charts. For example, if you want to see a basic high-low-close-volume bar chart for IBM for a 90-day period, the program will require 450 items of data. Although you can manually enter this data into the computer via the keyboard, most programs have the ability to obtain the required data from an on-line service, such as Dow Jones News/Retrieval. This method of retrieval will greatly reduce the time needed to create a chart and, if you wish, enable you to expand the number of stocks you follow.

Three factors distinguish one on-line service from another: the types of historical pricing information that are available on the on-line service, the time period for which information is available, and the format of the historical prices.

Some on-line services contain historical prices for stocks only. Others have historical pricing information available for stocks, bonds, mutual funds, market indices, and commodities (see Exhibit 11–1). The type of data you want to analyze is an important consideration in selecting an on-line service.

Another important consideration is the length of time for which data is available. For example, Dow Jones News/Retrieval has only one year of daily historical prices available for stocks, whereas Warner Computer Services has 10 years of daily data.

Finally, the data format is critical. There are three primary data formats used by technical analysis software. They are Dow Jones (also known as RTR), CompuTrac, and CSI (Commodity Systems, Inc.) formats. The historical database you use probably will depend on the data format the software package you use requires.

EXHIBIT 11–1 Sources of Historical Pricing Information

	Stocks	Bonds	Mutual Funds	Market Indices	Options	Commodities
	\multicolumn{6}{Historical Prices}					
Commodity Systems, Inc.	X			X	X	X
CompuServe	X	X	X	X	X	X
Dow Jones News/Retrieval	X			X		
Merlin Dial/Data	X	X	X	X	X	X
Nite-Line	X	X		X	X	X
Warner Computer Systems	X	X	X	X	X	

DOW JONES NEWS/RETRIEVAL

Historical pricing information on Dow Jones News/Retrieval is limited to one year of daily quotes for common and preferred stocks and warrants. No historical prices are available for bonds, mutual funds, market indices (other than Dow Jones), options, or commodities.

WARNER COMPUTER SYSTEMS

Warner Computer Systems offers investors historical prices on over 50,000 securities. Daily historical prices are available for most securities dating back to January 1, 1975. In addition to equity issues, bonds, and mutual funds, you can access historical data for over 100 stock market indices, such as the Dow Jones Industrial Average, the New York Stock Exchange Composite, the Standard & Poor's 100 (OEX), and the Standard & Poor's 500.

COMPUSERVE

The Historical Pricing feature on CompuServe consists of 10 years of daily trading statistics and descriptive information on over 50,000 stocks, bonds, mutual funds, government issues, and options from major U.S. and Canadian exchanges. Also included are major market and industry indices including the New York Stock Exchange Composite, Value Line, Dow Jones Industrial Average, Standard & Poor's 500, Standard & Poor's Industry Composites, and Moody's. Five years of daily commodity price quotations are also available.

COMMODITY SYSTEMS, INC.

Commodity Systems, Inc. (CSI), is a comprehensive on-line source of commodity data. Through CSI, you can access current and historical pricing information for over 200 commodities including those traded on the Chicago Board of Trade, Chicago Mercantile Exchange, Coffee, Sugar and Cocoa Exchange, COMEX, Kansas City Board of Trade, Mid-America Commodity Exchange, Minneapolis Grain Exchange, New York Cotton Exchange, New York Futures Exchange, New York Mercantile Exchanges, and various exchanges in Hong Kong, London, Paris, Singapore, Sydney, Tokyo, and Winnipeg. The amount of historical data for each commodity ranges from 1 year to over 20 years, with most commodities traded on U.S. exchanges having approximately 20 years of data.

MERLIN DIAL/DATA

The Merlin Dial/Data database offers the investor a low-cost on-line source of current and historical pricing information for stocks, bonds, rights, warrants, government issues, mutual funds, options, indices, and commodities. Up to 15 years of historical prices can be retrieved for stocks traded on the New York Stock Exchange, American Stock Exchange, and over-the-counter. In addition, up to 20 years of historical data is available for contracts traded on virtually every commodity exchange.

NITE-LINE®

Another on-line service providing historical pricing information is Nite-Line. It offers up to nine months of historical data on stocks, bonds, options, and indices, and up to two years of historical data for all major commodities traded on U.S. and London exchanges.

PROGRAMS FOR RETRIEVING HISTORICAL PRICES

Many technical analysis software packages include the capability to access an on-line service and automatically retrieve data in the format required by the software. Others assume you already have the data in the format used by the software.

Two good software packages that have been designed exclusively to retrieve current and historical pricing information are The Downloader™ and Quicktrieve.™ The Downloader from Computer Asset Management enables you to retrieve data from Warner Computer Systems in CompuTrac format.

Quicktrieve from Commodity Systems, Inc. (CSI), allows you to retrieve data from CSI's on-line service in CSI format. Then, if you wish, you can use one of Quicktrieve's utility programs to convert the CSI formatted data to CompuTrac or Dow Jones format. You can also create ASCII files that can be read by spreadsheet programs, such as Lotus 1-2-3. The utility programs are particularly valuable because they enable you to perform analysis with several different software packages without incurring the expense of retrieving the same data over and over again in different formats.

CONCLUSION

Historical pricing information is essential to the proper utilization of technical analysis software. It also represents an ongoing cost that must be controlled. Evaluate the on-line services and retrieval software packages carefully to ensure that you will be able to retrieve the specific types of data you want to analyze and control your ongoing costs.

PART 5

Options

CHAPTER 12

Options Analysis

During the past few years, the use of options as an investment vehicle has increased dramatically. Investors can now buy options on hundreds of stocks, stock indices, futures, bonds, and currency.

Investors use options to earn extra income on the securities they own or to hedge their positions and protect against drops in the prices of the securities they own. In addition, those inclined to accept the risk use the leverage options offer for speculative purposes.

An option is the right to buy or sell a specific number of shares, usually 100, at a fixed price within a set period of time. The fixed price is known as the strike price, and the date the right to buy or sell the shares ends is called the expiration date.

There are two types of options that you can buy, a call and a put. A call gives you the right to buy a specified number of shares at a fixed price within a set period of time. A put enables you to sell a specified number of shares at a fixed price within a set period of time.

Options are used for a variety of reasons, but the primary one is to take advantage of the high leverage associated with them. For example, suppose you expect the price of the shares of XYZ Corporation to rise significantly during the next few months. You can buy the stock for $100 per share or call options for $5 having a strike price of $100 that expires in three months.

Buying 100 shares of XYZ Corporation will cost you $10,000. Buying a call option that gives you the right to buy 100 shares of XYZ Corporation at any time during the next three months will cost you $500.

What happens if the price of the stock goes up, say to $120 per share, by the expiration date? The 100 shares of stock will be worth $12,000 for a 20 percent gain. Not bad, but look what the options will do. They will be worth $2,000, for a profit of $1,500 or 300 percent on the initial investment.

This all sounds good, but what happens if you are wrong and the stock goes down in price to $95 per share by the expiration date? The 100 shares of stock will be worth $9,500, a 5 percent loss. On the other hand, the options will be worthless, a 100 percent loss.

The leverage associated with options is spectacular. If you are right about the direction a stock is going to move, you can make a great deal of money. But if you are wrong, you stand to lose a significant portion of your investment.

In addition to simply buying a call or put option, there are many complex option strategies that involve various combinations of call and put options and the underlying security. A discussion of these strategies is beyond the scope of this book. If you are interested in learning more about option strategies, read a good book on options.

SELECTING OPTIONS SOFTWARE

Numerous factors should be considered when selecting an options software package that will meet your individual needs. A good way to compare your alternatives is to complete a questionnaire similar to the one provided in Exhibit 12–1 for each package. By doing so, you will ensure that you have entertained all of the important considerations in evaluating options software. For illustrative purposes, Exhibit 12–2 shows a completed options software questionnaire for OpVal Advanced Version.

Most options software packages use a few items of input (namely, the option's strike price, price of the underlying security, time left until expiration, short-term interest rate, and the volatility of the underlying security) to calculate theoretical values for call and put options, hedge ratios (or deltas), and implied volatility. The objective is to find specific buy and sell opportunities offering the highest risk-adjusted return.

The option valuation models used by the various options software packages to value options differ significantly. In fact, it is possible to evaluate the same option using three different software packages and arrive at three different conclusions regarding its valuation (undervalued, overvalued, and fairly valued).

EXHIBIT 12–1 Options Software Questionnaire—IBM PC Systems

GENERAL INFORMATION

Product name: _____ Version #: _____
Vendor name: _____
Address: _____
_____
_____

Telephone: _____
List price: _____
Demonstration diskette available? _____ Yes _____ No
  If yes, what is the price of the demonstration diskette? _____
Money-back guarantee available? _____ Yes _____ No
  If yes, how many days? _____

HARDWARE REQUIREMENTS
Operating system: _____ DOS 1.1 or later _____Other (Specify) _____
  _____ DOS 2.0 or later
Minimum memory required: _____ 64K _____ 128K _____ 192K _____ 256K
Number of disk drives required: _____ 1 singled-sided
  _____ 2 single-sided
  _____ 1 double-sided
  _____ 2 double-sided
  Other _____
Color graphics required? _____ Yes _____ No
Modem required? _____ Yes _____ No
Modem recommended? _____ Yes _____ No
Printer required? _____ Yes _____ No
Printer recommended? _____ Yes _____ No
Other hardware requirements (specify): _____
_____
_____
_____

PRODUCT SUPPORT
Who provides support for the product? _____
Is there a telephone number available for support? _____ Yes _____ No
  If yes, is it toll-free? _____ Yes _____ No
  Days of the week support is available: _____
  Hours of the day support is available: _____
Is the software copy protected? _____ Yes _____ No
  If yes, can you copy program to a hard disk? _____ Yes _____ No
  Cost of backup copy? _____
Defective disk replacement policy: _____
_____
_____
_____

Update policy: _____
_____
_____
_____

EXHIBIT 12–1 (*Continued*)

DOCUMENTATION

Number of pages in user's manual? _____

User's manual includes: Yes   No
- Tutorial _____ _____
- Index _____ _____
- Glossary _____ _____
- Explanation of error messages _____ _____
- Sample applications _____ _____
- Samples of screen displays _____ _____
- Samples of printed output _____ _____

Does the package include a tutorial on disk? _____ Yes _____ No
Does the package include a reference card? _____ Yes _____ No
Does the disk contain sample applications? _____ Yes _____ No
    If yes, how many and what type? _____
Does the package include a demonstration disk? _____ Yes _____ No

EASE OF USE

Estimated time to learn basic functions:
    ____ Less than 1 day   ____ 1 to 6 days   ____ 1 to 2 weeks
    ____ Over 2 weeks

Commands are abbreviated for quick entry? _____ Yes _____ No
Error messages are provided on screen? _____ Yes _____ No
Programs are menu driven? _____ Yes _____ No
Help screens are available? _____ At all times
                                    _____ At various points in the program
                                    _____ Nonexistent

How experienced with the IBM PC should a person be to use this package?
    ____ Very   ____ Somewhat   ____ Little   ____ No experience

OPTIONS ANALYZED

Which of the following types of options can be analyzed? (Check all that apply)
    _____ Stock options
    _____ Options on stock indices
    _____ Options on futures
    _____ Cash bond options
    _____ Currency options

OPTION STRATEGIES

Which of the following types of option strategies can be analyzed? (Check all that apply)

_____ Long call	_____ Long straddle
_____ Short call	_____ Short straddle
_____ Long put	_____ Long strangle
_____ Short put	_____ Short strangle
_____ Bull spread	_____ Call ratio spread
_____ Bear spread	_____ Put ratio spread
_____ Long butterfly	_____ Call ratio backspread
_____ Short butterfly	_____ Put ratio backspread
_____ Long condor	_____ Box or conversion
_____ Short condor	_____ Other (Specify) _____

EXHIBIT 12–1 (Continued)

DATA ENTRY

Is the user prompted for data to be entered? _____ Yes _____ No
Which of the following items are entered? (Check all that apply)
_____ Current date
_____ Type of underlying security
_____ Current price of the underlying security
_____ Call or put
_____ Quantity
_____ Strike price of the options
_____ Option expiration date
_____ Options cycle (Jan, Feb, Mar)
_____ Risk-free interest rate
_____ Volatility of the underlying security
_____ Ex-dividend date
_____ Expected dividend payments
_____ Holding costs
_____ Other (Specify) _____
Can the user access an on-line database for current price updates?
_____ Yes _____ No
If yes, which on-line database is accessed? (Check all that apply)
_____ Dow Jones News/Retrieval
_____ Warner Computer Systems
_____ Other (Specify) _____
_____ Other (Specify) _____
Does the software allow for entry of fractional prices? _____ Yes _____ No
After data is entered, can it be easily checked and changed?
_____ Yes _____ No

FEATURES

Which of the following option valuation models are used? (Check all that apply)
_____ Black-Scholes Option Pricing Model
_____ Parkinson Model
_____ Fischer Black (Futures)
_____ Fischer Black (Physical)
_____ Cox-Ross-Rubenstein
_____ Cleeton
_____ Other (Specify) _____
Which of the following calculations are performed on data entered? (Check all
that apply)
_____ Theoretical values for options
_____ Hedge ratios (or deltas)
_____ Implied volatility
_____ Days to expiration
_____ Expected return and risk of position
_____ Commission costs
_____ Expected value of a position at different dates, volatilities, and
underlying instrument values
_____ Other (Specify) _____
_____ Other (Specify) _____

EXHIBIT 12–1 (*Concluded*)

Can a portfolio of securities and options be stored on a disk for later
examination? _____ Yes _____ No
If yes, what is the maximum number of portfolios that can be created? _____

If yes, what is the maximum number of positions that can be included
within a portfolio? _____

REPORTS AND GRAPHS

Can reports be generated on the screen? _____ Yes _____ No
Can reports be printed? _____ Yes _____ No
Which of the following types of reports and graphs can be generated? (Check
all that apply)
_____ Table of days to expiration
_____ Table of fair prices for options
_____ Position table
_____ Table of market prices for options
_____ Table of expected profits and losses
_____ Table of implied volatility of options
_____ Graph of position value versus stock price
_____ Graph of position value versus time
_____ Other (Specify) _____
_____ Other (Specify) _____
Which of the following items do reports display? (Check all that apply)
_____ Days to expiration
_____ Fair price of options
_____ Positions
_____ Market price of options
_____ Implied volatility
_____ Hedge ratio
_____ Risk/reward ratio
_____ Other (Specify) _____
_____ Other (Specify) _____

EXHIBIT 12–2 Completed Options Software Questionnaire for OpVal
Advanced Version—IBM PC Version

GENERAL INFORMATION

Product name: OpVal Advanced Version   Version #: 1.5
Vendor name: CalcShop Inc.
Address: Box 1231
West Caldwell, NJ 07007

Telephone: (201) 228–9139

EXHIBIT 12–2 *(Continued)*

List price: $250.00

Demonstration diskette available?   _____ Yes   _X_ No
    If yes, what is the price of the demonstration diskette? _____ N/A*

Money-back guarantee available?   _X_ Yes   _____ No
    If yes, how many days? _____

HARDWARE REQUIREMENTS

Operating system: _X_ DOS 1.1 or later   _____Other (Specify) _____
                          _____ DOS 2.0 or later

Minimum memory required: _____ 64K   _X_ 128K   _____ 192K   _____ 256K

Number of disk drives required: _X_ 1 singled-sided
                                           _____ 2 single-sided
                                           _____ 1 double-sided
                                           _____ 2 double-sided
                          Other _____

Color graphics required?   _____ Yes   _X_ No
Modem required?   _____ Yes   _X_ No
Modem recommended?   _X_ Yes   _____ No
Printer required?   _____ Yes   _X_ No
Printer recommended?   _X_ Yes   _____ No
Other hardware requirements (specify): None _____

_____
_____
_____
_____

PRODUCT SUPPORT

Who provides support for the product? _____ CalcShop Inc. _____
Is there a telephone number available for support? _X_ Yes _____ No
    If yes, is it toll-free?   _____ Yes   _X_ No
    Days of the week support is available: _____ Monday to Friday _____
    Hours of the day support is available: _____ Business hours _____
Is the software copy protected?   _X_ Yes   _____ No
    If yes, can you copy program to a hard disk?   _____ Yes   _X_ No
    Cost of backup copy? 1 backup copy provided with package
Defective disk replacement policy: CalcShop will replace defective disks
    for a period of 6 months from date of purchase. _____

_____
_____

Update policy: No update policy is indicated. _____

_____
_____

EXHIBIT 12–2 *(Continued)*

DOCUMENTATION

Number of pages in user's manual? ____78____
User's manual includes: Yes   No

	Yes	No
Tutorial	X	
Index		X
Glossary		X
Explanation of error messages		X
Sample applications		X
Samples of screen displays	X	
Samples of printed output	X	

Does the package include a tutorial on disk?   _____ Yes   _X_ No
Does the package include a reference card?   _____ Yes   _X_ No
Does the disk contain sample applications?   _____ Yes   _X_ No
    If yes, how many and what type? _____N/A_____
Does the package include a demonstration disk?   _____ Yes   _X_ No

EASE OF USE

Estimated time to learn basic functions:
    ____ Less than 1 day _X_ 1 to 6 days ____ 1 to 2 weeks
    ____ Over 2 weeks

Commands are abbreviated for quick entry?   _X_ Yes   _____ No
Error messages are provided on screen?   _X_ Yes   _____ No
Programs are menu driven?   _X_ Yes   ____ No
Help screens are available?   _____ At all times
                      _____ At various points in the program
                      _X_ Nonexistent
How experienced with the IBM PC should a person be to use this package?
    ____ Very ____ Somewhat _X_ Little ____ No experience

OPTIONS ANALYZED

Which of the following types of options can be analyzed? (Check all that apply)
    _X_ Stock options
    _X_ Options on stock indices
    _X_ Options on futures
    _____ Cash bond options
    _X_ Currency options

OPTION STRATEGIES

Which of the following types of option strategies can be analyzed? (Check all that apply)

_X_ Long call	_X_ Long straddle
_X_ Short call	_X_ Short straddle
_X_ Long put	_X_ Long strangle
_X_ Short put	_X_ Short strangle
_X_ Bull spread	_X_ Call ratio spread

EXHIBIT 12–2 (*Continued*)

_X_ Bear spread   _X_ Put ratio spread
_X_ Long butterfly   _X_ Call ratio backspread
_X_ Short butterfly   _X_ Put ratio backspread
_X_ Long condor   _X_ Box or conversion
_X_ Short condor   _X_ Other (Specify) Users can
evaluate any strategy
comprised of long or short
positions in up to 48
different series of calls and
48 different series of puts
and the underlying security.

DATA ENTRY

Is the user prompted for data to be entered?   _X_ Yes   ___ No
Which of the following items are entered? (Check all that apply)

_X_ Current date
___ Type of underlying security
_X_ Current price of the underlying security
_X_ Call or put
_X_ Quantity
_X_ Strike price of the options
___ Option expiration date
_X_ Options cycle (Jan, Feb, Mar)
_X_ Risk-free interest rate
_X_ Volatility of the underlying security
_X_ Ex-dividend date
_X_ Expected dividend payments
___ Holding costs
___ Other (Specify) _____

Can the user access an on-line database for current price updates?
_X_ Yes   ___ No
If yes, which on-line database is accessed? (Check all that apply)

_X_ Dow Jones News/Retrieval
_X_ Warner Computer Systems
___ Other (Specify) _____
___ Other (Specify) _____

Does the software allow for entry of fractional prices? _X_ Yes ___ No
After data is entered, can it be easily checked and changed?
_X_ Yes   ___ No

FEATURES

Which of the following option valuation models are used? (Check all that apply)

_X_ Black-Scholes Option Pricing Model
___ Parkinson Model
___ Fischer Black (Futures)
___ Fischer Black (Physical)
___ Cox-Ross-Rubenstein

EXHIBIT 12–2 (*Concluded*)

_____ Cleeton
_____ Other (Specify) _____

Which of the following calculations are performed on data entered? (Check all that apply)

__X__ Theoretical values for options

__X__ Hedge ratios (or deltas)

__X__ Implied volatility

__X__ Days to expiration

__X__ Expected return and risk of position

__X__ Commission costs

__X__ Expected value of a position at different dates, volatilities, and underlying instrument values

_____ Other (Specify) _____

_____ Other (Specify) _____

Can a portfolio of securities and options be stored on a disk for later examination?   __X__ Yes   _____ No

If yes, what is the maximum number of portfolios that can be created? Unlimited

If yes, what is the maximum number of positions that can be included within a portfolio? _____ 96 _____

REPORTS AND GRAPHS

Can reports be generated on the screen?   __X__ Yes   _____ No

Can reports be printed?   __X__ Yes   _____ No

Which of the following types of reports and graphs can be generated? (Check all that apply)

__X__ Table of days to expiration

__X__ Table of fair prices for options

__X__ Position table

__X__ Table of market prices for options

__X__ Table of expected profits and losses

__X__ Table of implied volatility of options

__X__ Graph of position value versus stock price

__X__ Graph of position value versus time

_____ Other (Specify) _____

_____ Other (Specify) _____

Which of the following items do reports display? (Check all that apply)

__X__ Days to expiration

__X__ Fair price of options

__X__ Positions

__X__ Market price of options

__X__ Implied volatility

__X__ Hedge ratio

_____ Risk/reward ratio

__X__ Other (Specify) Expected profit _____

_____ Other (Specify) _____

*N/A = not applicable.

When selecting an options software package, it is critical that you know what option valuation model (i.e., Black-Scholes Option Pricing Model) is being used by the software. Furthermore, since the various option valuation models can produce significantly different results, you need to understand the theory behind a given model and whether it is legitimate given the type of options you intend to analyze.

To give you an idea of what you can accomplish using an options software package, let's take a look at a typical package, OpVal.

USING A TYPICAL OPTIONS SOFTWARE PACKAGE

OpVal is designed to analyze simple and complex investment strategies involving stock, index, and futures options, as well as warrants and convertibles. The program allows you to forecast up to 96 Black-Scholes prices in just five seconds.

OpVal is set up like an electronic book with information divided into logical categories and displayed like the pages of a book. When you load the program, the table of contents appears on the screen. As with standard menus, you type a two-letter page code to go to a specific page, such as FT to go to the fair price table page or ET to go to the expected profit table page.

The information required by OpVal is entered on four different pages, namely the date and rate page, the stock or index data page, the position table page, and the market price table page. On the date and rate page, you enter the current date and the prevailing interest rate on short-term Treasury bills. The current price, annual dividend, and volatility of the underlying security, as well as the options cycle are entered on the stock or index data page.

The position table page, as illustrated in Exhibit 12–3, is basically a matrix with strike prices shown vertically and calls and puts for various expiration dates shown horizontally. To enter a position, you simply move the cursor to the intersection of the strike price and the appropriate call or put expiration date and type in the number of contracts that you want evaluated. You indicate contracts that are short with a minus sign. In addition, the position in the underlying security is entered at the bottom of the position table page.

EXHIBIT 12–3 Sample Position Table Page

```
                     POSITION TABLE                   PT= PG  6
                 CALLS                      PUTS
  STRIKE   JUN 17 83 SEP 16 83 DEC 16 83 JUN 17 83 SEP 16 83 DEC 16 83
  # # #
  # # #
  # # #
  45         0         0         0         0        10         0
  50         0        -2         0         0         0         0
  55         0         0         0         0         0         0
  # # #
  # # #
  # # #
  # # #
  # # #
  # # #
  # # #
  # # #
  # # #

SHARES ? L5


     SAMPLE   P50 1/4   D2        V35       JUN 7 83 I9.8
          #### Press <Home> for Help Screen. ####
```

OpVal allows you to enter positions in one security and up to 48 different calls and 48 different puts, thus enabling you to evaluate virtually any simple or complex option strategy.

OpVal uses the information in the rate and date page, stock or index data page, and the position table page to forecast position values and position share equivalents, as well as to prepare graphs and tables of expected profit or loss due to changes in the underlying security price or changes in the time to expiration.

Finally, the market price table is used for entry of actual market prices, which are subsequently used by OpVal to calculate the expected profit from positions in each option, the net expected profit from a set of positions, and the implied volatility of the underlying security. Market prices can be entered manually or automatically via Dow Jones News/Retrieval or Warner Computer Systems.

EXHIBIT 12–4   Graph of Position Value versus Time

```
                    GRAPH VS TIME              GT= PG 11

V RANGE? $1000    VG ZERO? $25781    VT ZERO? $25781    FAR INV =$25781
H RANGE? W16      PRICE C? $ # # #   NT COST? $0        FAR EQT =$25571
1   +                               WEEKS   VALUE CHG  WEEKS    FAR RLZ
    !                               0       -420.2     0        25361
.75 +                               1       -465.6     1        25315
    !                               2       -525.1     2        25256
.5  +                               3       -558.4     3        25223
    !                               4       -609.7     4        25171
.25 +                               5       -661       5        25120
    !                               6       -708.3     6        25073
0   +---+---+---+---+---+---+---+    7       -755.5     7        25025
    !                               8       -808.7     8        24972
.25 +                               9       -869.8     9        24911
    #                               10      -926.9     10       24854
.5  + # # #                         11      -977.9     11       24803
    !       # #                     12      -1020.7    12       24760
.75 +         # # #                 13      -1026.3    13       24755
    !           # #      # # #       14      -908.2     14       24873
1   +               # # #           15      -857.3     15       24924
    0     4     8    12    16 16     16      -857.3     16       24924

              P50 1/4   D2      V35      JUN 7 83 19.8
              #### Press <Home> for Help Screen. ####
```

OpVal incorporates the dividend adjusted Black-Scholes Model to evaluate calls and puts. Rather than using the actual historical volatility figures used by the original Black-Scholes Model, however, OpVal applies market implied volatility, an estimate of the underlying security's future volatility. The estimate of future volatility is computed from the market prices of the options as entered on the market price table page.

All option pages of OpVal are laid out like the option tables in *The Wall Street Journal*—horizontal by month, vertical by strike price. Hedge ratios (deltas) are shown in the same fashion. Hedge ratios can be calculated for a single option or a complex position.

Option positions can be illustrated with two types of graphs (see Exhibits 12–4 and 12–5). One graph helps you visualize leverage by showing how price changes in the underlying security

EXHIBIT 12–5 Graph of Position Value versus Stock Price

```
                    GRAPH VS STOCK                  GS= PG 10

V RANGE? $4000     VG ZERO? $25781    VT ZERO? $25781    FAR INV =$25781
H RANGE? $16       TIME CH? W4        NT COST? $0        FAR EQT =$25571
4                  +              *   PRICE CHG VALUE CHG PRICE    FAR RLZ
                   !                    -16      1879.8   34 1/4   27661
3                  +            *        -14      885.1   36 1/4   26666
                   !         *           -12      35      38 1/4   25816
2  *               +       *             -10     -539.5   40 1/4   25241
                   !     *                -8     -916.8   42 1/4   24864
1    *             +    *                 -6    -1096.5   44 1/4   24684
                   !  *                   -4    -1096.7   46 1/4   24684
0  +---*---+---+---+-*-+---+---+---+-     -2     -917     48 1/4   24864
         *         *                       * * *  -609.7  50 1/4   25171
1          * * * * +                       2     -193.15 52 1/4   25588
                   !                       4      286.77 54 1/4   26068
2                  +                       6      816.2  56 1/4   26597
                   !                       8     1380.6  58 1/4   27162
3                  +                      10     1961.6  60 1/4   27743
                   !                      12     2558.6  62 1/4   28340
4                  +                      14     3171    64 1/4   28952
     16 12  8  4   0  4  8  12 16 16      3782           66 1/4   29563

                P50 1/4   D2       V35       JUN 7 83 I9.8
                **** Press <Home> for Help Screen. ****
```

affect an option position, while the other illustrates the effect of time on an option position.

An important feature of OpVal is its capability to include the effect of commissions in all calculations. It can handle both full and discount brokerage fees.

CONCLUSION

OpVal illustrates what you can do with a typical options software package. Like other options software, it can be used to evaluate simple and complex option strategies using a specific option valuation model.

The specific option valuation model used is the key to being able to benefit from options software. Make sure the package you select uses an option valuation model that is appropriate for the underlying instrument (i.e., stocks, stock indices, futures, etc.) being analyzed.

APPENDIX A
Staying Current

Investment software is in a constant state of change. New software packages are constantly being introduced into the marketplace, while some software packages on the market are improved and others are taken off the market.

The capabilities of investment software will increase substantially as time goes on. By keeping up to date on these capabilities, you can maintain an edge over other investors and increase your potential for realizing a greater return on your investments.

Publications

Keeping abreast of advances in investment software and on-line services can be very beneficial to the serious investor. The following publications provide valuable current information.

Computerized Investing
American Association of Individual Investors, Inc.
612 N. Michigan Street
Chicago, IL 60611
Note: On an annual basis the American Association of Individual Investors, Inc. publishes *The Individual Investor's Microcomputer Resource Guide*. It contains detailed descriptions of most of the investment software products and on-line services of interest to the individual investor.

Better Investing BITS
National Association of Investors Corporation
1515 E. Eleven Mile Road
Royal Oak, MI 48067

Wall Street Computer Review
150 Broadway
New York, NY 10038

Wall Street Micro Investor
9th Floor
11 Hanover Square
New York, NY 10005

In addition, other general computer publications frequently print reviews of investment software products. Five magazines that are of particular value are:

InfoWorld
CW Communications
1060 Marsh Rd., Suite C-200
Menlo Park, CA 94052

PC Magazine
Ziff-Davis Publishing Company
One Park Avenue
New York, NY 10016

PC Week
Ziff-Davis Publishing Company
15 Crawford St.
Needham, MA 02194

PC World
PC World Communications, Inc.
555 De Haro St.
San Francisco, CA 94107

Personal Computing
Hayden Publishing Co.
10 Mulholland Dr.
Hasbrouck Heights, NJ 07604

APPENDIX B
Investment Software

CompuTrac/PC
CompuTrac, Inc.
Technical Analysis Group
P.O. Box 15951
New Orleans, LA 70175
(800) 535-7990; (504) 895-1474 (In Louisiana)
System(s): IBM PC
List price: $1,900

Dow Jones Spreadsheet Link
Dow Jones & Co., Inc.
P.O. Box 300
Princeton, NJ 08543
(800) 257-5114; (609) 452-1511 (In New Jersey)
System(s): Apple II series, Apple Macintosh, IBM PC
List price: $249 for Apple II series and IBM PC,
         $99 for Apple Macintosh

The Downloader
Computer Asset Management
P.O. Box 26743
Salt Lake City, UT 84126
(800) 882-3040; (801) 964-0391 (In Utah)
System(s): IBM PC
List price: $49

The Equalizer
Schwab's Investor Information Service
Charles Schwab & Co., Inc.
101 Montgomery Street
San Francisco, CA 94104
(800) 334-4455
System(s): Apple II series, IBM PC
List price: $199

The Evaluation Form
Investor's Software
Box N
Bradenton Beach, FL 33510
(813) 778-5515

System(s): Apple II series, IBM PC
List price: $100

Lotus 1-2-3
Lotus Development Corporation
55 Cambridge Parkway
Cambridge, MA 02142
(617) 577-8500
System(s): IBM PC
List price: $495

Market Link
Smith Micro Software, Inc.
P.O. Box 7137
Huntington Beach, CA 92615
(714) 964-0412
System(s): Apple Macintosh, IBM PC
List price: $85

MetaStock
Computer Asset Management
P.O. Box 26743
Salt Lake City, UT 84126
(800) 882-3040; (801) 964-0391 (In Utah)
System(s): IBM PC
List price: $195

OpVal Advanced Version
CalcShop, Inc.
P.O. Box 1231
West Caldwell, NJ 07007
(201) 228-9139
System(s): Apple II series, IBM PC
List price: $250

ProfitTaker
Investment Growth Corporation
1430 W. Busch Blvd., Suite 4
Tampa, FL 33612
(813) 933-1164
System(s): Apple II series, IBM PC
List price: $795 for Apple II series, $995 for IBM PC

Quicktrieve
Commodity Systems, Inc.

200 W. Palmetto Park Road
Boca Raton, FL 33432
(800) 327-0175 or (305) 392-8663 (In Florida)
System(s): Apple II series, IBM PC
List price: Free with $150 subscription to Commodity
              Systems on-line service

Stockpak II
Standard & Poor's Corporation
Micro Services Dept.
25 Broadway
New York, NY 10004
(800) 852-5200; (212) 208-8581 (In New York)
System(s): Apple II series, IBM PC
List price: $275 to $520 per year depending upon
            subscription

Stock Portfolio System
Smith Micro Software, Inc.
P.O. Box 7137
Huntington Beach, CA 92615
(714) 964-0412
System(s): Apple II series, Apple Macintosh, IBM PC
List price: $185 for Apple II series,
            $225 for Apple Macintosh and IBM PC

The Technician
Computer Asset Management
P.O. Box 26743
Salt Lake City, UT 84126
(800) 882-3040; (801) 964-0391 (In Utah)
System(s): IBM PC
List price: $395

Telescan Analyzer
Telescan, Inc.
11011 Richmond Ave., Suite 600
Houston, TX 77042
(800) 624-9307; (713) 952-1060
System(s): IBM PC
List price: $49.95

Value/Screen Plus
Value Line, Inc.

711 Third Ave.
New York, NY 10017
(212) 687-3965
System(s): Apple II series, IBM PC

List price: Monthly subscription is $348 per year;
quarterly subscription is $211 for the first year and
$116 for a renewal

APPENDIX C
On-Line Services

Commodity Systems, Inc.
200 W. Palmetto Park Road
Boca Raton, Fl 33432
(800) 327-0175 or (305) 392-8663
Registration fee: $150 (includes a communications software
package)
Minimum monthly usage fee: $26

CompuServe Information Service
5000 Arlington Centre Boulevard
Columbus, OH 43220
(800) 848-8990 or (614) 457-8650
Registration fee: $39.95 (basic service); $49.95 (with Executive
Service Option)
Minimum monthly usage fee: None (basic service); $10 (with Ex-
ecutive Service Option)

Dow Jones News/Retrieval
Dow Jones & Co., Inc.
P.O. Box 300
Princeton, NJ 08543
(800) 257-5114 or (609) 452-1511
Registration fee: $29.95
Minimum monthly usage fee: None

Merlin Dial/Data
Hale Systems, Inc.
1044 Northern Boulevard
Roslyn, NY 11576
(800) 645-3120 or (516) 484-4545
Registration fee: None
Minimum monthly usage fee: $15

Nite-Line
National Computer Network
1929 N. Harlem Avenue
Chicago, IL 60635
(312) 622-6666
Registration fee: $30
Minimum monthly user fee: None

Schwab's Investor Information Service
Charles Schwab & Co., Inc.
101 Montgomery Street
San Francisco, CA 94104
(800) 334-4455
Registration fee: None (Service requires usage of The Equalizer
           software - $199)
Minimum monthly usage fee: None

The Source
1616 Anderson Road
McLean, VA 22102
(800) 336-3366 or (703) 821-6666
Registration fee: $49.95
Minimum monthly usage fee: $10

Telescan
11011 Richmond Avenue
Suite 600
Houston, TX 77042
(800) 624-9307
Registration fee: None (Service requires usage of Telescan Ana-
           lyzer software - $49.95)
Minimum monthly usage fee: None

Warner Computer Systems, Inc.
One University Plaza
Hackensack, NJ 07601
(800) 626-4634 or (201) 489-1580
Registration fee: $48
Minimum monthly usage fee: None

GLOSSARY

ASCII The American Standard Code for Information Interchange (ASCII) is a standard data format. Data stored on disks in ASCII format can be read by various word processing and other types of programs. Data can be exchanged between programs that read data in ASCII format.

Asset An asset is anything of value owned by a company. Assets normally include cash, inventory, land, buildings, equipment, etc.

Baud The baud rate is the speed of transmission of data. For example, data is frequently transmitted over telephone lines using a modem at 1200 baud.

Balance Sheet A balance sheet is a financial statement showing what a company owns (assets), what it owes (liabilities), and the difference (stockholders' equity).

Beta Wall Street uses the second letter of the Greek alphabet, beta, to describe the volatility of a stock's price relative to the overall stock market. If a stock has a beta greater than 1, the stock is more volatile than the overall stock market. A beta of less than 1 indicates that the stock is less volatile than the overall stock market.

Bond A bond is a long-term debt obligation of a company. Generally, interest is paid to the bondholder at a set rate until the principal amount is repaid on the maturity date.

Book Value Book value represents the equity value of an outstanding share of stock. Book value is calculated by dividing stockholders' equity by the number of shares outstanding.

Bottom A bottom is a low for a stock or the overall market.

Breakout A substantial rise in price above a resistance level or decline in price below a support level is a breakout. When a breakout occurs, it is likely that the trend in price will continue.

Capital Gain/Loss The difference between the purchase and sale price of a security. If the purchase price is less than the sale price, it is a capital gain. If the purchase price is greater than the sale price, it is a capital loss.

Commission The commission is the fee charged by a stockbroker for buying and selling securities on behalf of a customer.

Commodity A commodity is one of a select group of items traded on one of the commodity exchanges for either immediate or future delivery. Examples of commodities are corn, sugar, cotton, cattle, gold, and silver.

Common Stock Common stock represents ownership of a corporation. Generally, common stockholders have voting rights that allow them to control management and company policy.

Current Asset A current asset is an item of value owned by a company that either is cash or is expected to be used up or converted to cash within one year. Current assets normally include cash, marketable securities, accounts receivable, inventory, etc.

Current Liability A current liability is any obligation of a company that will become due within one year. Current liabilities normally include accounts payable, the current portion of long-term debt, and taxes payable.

Current Ratio The current ratio is a common measure of a company's liquidity. It is calculated by dividing current assets by current liabilities.

Current Yield The current yield is expressed as a percentage and is calculated by dividing the annual dividend per share by the current market price of that stock.

Cycle A cycle is a price pattern or movement that regularly occurs in a given time interval. During each cycle there is a low point known as the *cycle low* and a high point known as the *cycle high.*

Debt to Equity Ratio The debt to equity ratio is a common measure of leverage in a company's financial structure. It is calculated by adding long-term debt to the par value of preferred stock and dividing that total by common stockholders' equity.

Disk A disk can be a floppy or hard disk. A floppy disk is a flexible magnetic recording medium partially encased by a plastic cover. A hard disk is not flexible and is completely encased. More information can be stored on a hard disk than on a floppy disk.

Disk Drive A disk drive is used to read and write information on a disk.

Dividends Dividends represent payments to stockholders of a portion of a company's profits. Often, stockholders receive dividends on a quarterly basis.

Earnings per Share Earnings per share is the net earnings of a company divided by the number of outstanding shares of stock.

Ex-Dividend Date   Dividends are paid to stockholders owning shares as of a specified date prior to the actual date they are paid. That specified date is known as the ex-dividend date.

Fundamental Analysis   Fundamental analysis is based on the belief that stock prices are determined by the underlying value of a company in terms of its cash, current assets, and earnings.

Hardware   The components of a computer system, such as the system unit, keyboard, monitor, printer, and so forth. Hardware is used to execute instructions given by software.

Income Statement.   An income statement is a financial statement that presents a company's revenues, expenses, and earnings over a specific period of time, usually quarterly or annually.

Liability   A liability is anything a company owes.

Long-Term   As defined by the Internal Revenue Service, holding securities for a period greater than six months qualifies those securities for long-term status that receives a more favorable tax treatment.

Margin   Buying securities on margin involves using securities purchased with cash as collateral for additional securities that are purchased with money borrowed from a stockbroker.

Memory   Memory is where information is stored. Information stored temporarily on a microchip in the system unit is known as random access memory (RAM). Information stored on a disk is known as read only memory (ROM).

Modem   A modem is a device that allows you to send and receive information over telephone lines.

Moving Averages   Individual stock prices can fluctuate widely from day to day making it difficult to determine the trend of a security's price. For that reason, technical analysts use moving averages to smooth over daily price fluctuations. Three basic types of moving averages are used in technical analysis: simple, weighted, and exponential.

Simple   A simple moving average is calculated by adding data, usually daily or weekly, for a set period of time and dividing the total by the number of periods. For example, a 10-day simple moving average of a stock's price is calculated by summing each day's price for 10 days and dividing by 10.

Weighted   A weighted moving average is calculated by averaging data over a set period of time giving more emphasis to the most recent data. For example, a 10-day weighted moving average of a stock's price could be calculated by giving the oldest day's price a weight of 1, the next day's price a weight of 2, and so on, with the current day's price given a weight of 10. You multiply each day's price by its weight, add the products together, and divide by the total of the weights, which is 55 in this case.

Exponential Like a weighted moving average, an exponential moving average gives greater weight to more recent data. However, it is easier to calculate on a regular basis. Calculating an exponential moving average is a two-step process. First, you multiply the difference between the current period's price and the exponential moving average for the previous period by an exponent, which varies depending on the length of the moving average. Secondly, you add the product of that calculation to the previous exponential moving average to arrive at the current period's exponential moving average.

Mutual Fund A mutual fund is a professionally managed portfolio of securities. Investors buy and sell shares of the fund, thus benefiting from the lower risk that is often associated with a diversified portfolio of securities.

On-Balance Volume On-balance volume is a technical indicator that manipulates volume figures to measure accumulation and distribution of a stock. Accumulation is indicated by rising on-balance volume; distribution by falling on-balance volume.

Optimization Optimization procedures are performed on historical data to determine the value of one indicator or combination of values of multiple indicators which would have resulted in the maximum profit during a given period of time.

Option An option is a speculative market instrument representing the right to buy or sell a stock at a fixed price within a specified time. Call options represent the right to buy, while put options represent the right to sell.

Oscillator An oscillator is the difference between two moving averages.

Overbought Overbought is a term used to describe a condition that occurs after a period of vigorous buying. It is a point at which upward momentum in prices can no longer be maintained and therefore the prices will stay at the same level or go down.

Oversold Oversold is the opposite of overbought. It is a point at which downward momentum in prices can no longer be maintained and therefore the prices will stay at the same level or go up.

Point and Figure Chart   A point and figure chart records price activity without reference to time and volume. Point and figure charts are used to determine the trend in a security's price.

Portfolio   A portfolio is the investment holdings of an individual or company. By including a variety of stocks and bonds, as well as other investments, portfolios are designed to achieve income and capital gain objectives and, at the same time, minimize risk.

Preferred Stock   Preferred stock, like common stock, represents ownership of a corporation. Unlike common stockholders, preferred stockholders normally have no voting rights. However, they do receive a fixed annual dividend that must be paid before common stockholders receive anything.

Price/Earnings Ratio   The price/earnings ratio is commonly used to measure the reasonability of a stock's price. The price/earnings ratio is calculated by dividing the current market price of a stock by the earnings per share figure.

Program   A program is a set of instructions that tells the computer what to do.

Relative Strength   Relative strength is determined by comparing the performance of an individual stock or group of stocks to the overall market (a market index). Relative strength is normally used to select stocks that are likely to outperform the overall market.

Resistance Level   The resistance level represents a price at which sellers tend to sell in sufficient volume to lower the price of a security. For example, if on five occasions the price of a given stock has risen to around $50 per share and, on each occasion, the price has subsequently dropped, a technical analyst would consider $50 per share to be a resistance level for that stock.

Short Sale   A short sale is a trading technique typically used when you expect the price of a stock to decline. An investor sells borrowed shares and hopes to buy the same number of shares at a later date for a lower price, return them to the lender, and realize a profit.

Short-Term   As defined by the Internal Revenue Service, holding a security for less than six months qualifies those securities for short-term treatment.

Software   A set of instructions that tell the computer what to do. All programs are software.

Spreadsheet Program   A spreadsheet program is an electronic worksheet. Data can be entered into a grid of cells referenced by row and column coordinates. Formula can be entered to automatically manipulate data. Lotus 1-2-3 is an example of a spreadsheet program.

Stock Split   A stock split occurs when a company divides its shares into a greater or lesser number. For example, a two-for-one stock split means that for each share you currently own, you receive one additional share for a total of two shares. Normally, stock splits are used to reduce the price per share in order to increase the activity of the shares in the market.

Stockholders' Equity   Stockholders' equity is often called *net worth*. It represents the difference between total assets and total liabilities.

Support Level   The support level represents a price at which buyers tend to buy in sufficient volume to raise the price of a security. For example, if on five occasions the price of a given stock has dropped to around $20 per share and, on each occasion, the price has subsequently risen, a technical analyst would consider $20 per share to be a support level for that stock.

Technical Analysis   Technical analysis is the study of stocks and the overall market based on supply and demand. Technical analysts use charts of historical price and volume activity to predict future price movements.

Technical Indicator   A technical indicator uses historical price and volume data to forecast price movements of individual stocks, industry groups, and the overall market.

Ticker Symbol   A ticker symbol is a combination of letters used by the exchanges to identify a particular security. For example, the ticker symbol IBM is used to identify the common stock of International Business Machines.

Top   A top is a high for a stock or the overall market.

Trading Band (also Known as Envelope)   A trading band contains normal price fluctuations. It is shown graphically as parallel lines at certain percentage points above and below any field on display.

Treasury Bill   A Treasury bill is a short-term debt obligation of the U.S. Treasury that matures within one year.

Trend   The trend is the direction of a price movement.

Trendline   A trendline is a straight line on a chart that connects consecutive tops or consecutive bottoms. Trendlines are used to identify levels of support and resistance.

Volume Histogram   A volume histogram usually accompanies a high-low-close bar chart. Volume is shown at the bottom of the chart by a vertical bar under each period's price data.

Index